TURTLE TRUFFLE BARK!

TURTLE TRUFFLE BARK!

*simple and indulgent chocolates
to make at home*

HALLIE A. BAKER

COUNTRYMAN PRESS
NEW YORK, NY

The Countryman Press
Woodstock, Vermont
www.countrymanpress.com

A division of W. W. Norton & Company, Inc.,
500 Fifth Avenue, New York, NY 10110
www.wwnorton.com

For information about special discounts or bulk purchases, please contact
W.W. Norton Special Sales at specialsales@wwnorton.com or 800-233-4830.

Printed in The United States

ANF 3-27-15

Turtle, Truffle, Bark!
978-1-58157-285-8

Interior Design by Nick Caruso
All photos by Allan Penn, unless otherwise indicated below.

Page 20: © kjohansen/iStockphoto.com; 23: © aradaphotography/iStockphoto.com;
28: © LauriPatterson/iStockphoto.com; 33: © nathanphoto/iStockphoto.com; 48: © bhofack2/
iStockphoto.com; 55: ©mikafotostok/iStockphoto.com; 57: © Mny-Jhee/iStockphoto.com;
58: © dannyc23/iStockphoto.com; 67: © monkeybusinessimages/iStockcphoto.com;
76: © lambada/iStockphoto.com; 112: © Miuda_21/iStockphoto.com; 114: © AlexPro9500/
iStockphoto.com; 123: © ErikaMitchell/iStockphoto.com; 143: © Anna_Kurz/iStockphoto.com;
144: © Lilechka75/iStockphoto.com

10 9 8 7 6 5 4 3 2 1

This book is dedicated to my husband, Graham,
and to the memory of my mother and of my father,
who let me know I could do anything.

contents

BARKS

TURTLES

TRUFFLES

introduction

This is a book of dreams. Sweet dreams.

Chocolate and caramel had been a passion for me long before I began to work with them at age twenty-two. As a child, I had a wonderful grandmother who could cook anything, but sweets were her favorite. Dessert was never forgotten or tacked on to the end of the meal—it was an integral part of the whole experience. The family waited all year long for her dark chocolate almond crunch Christmas tins, then fought over the last pieces.

My grandmother Thelma whipped up her candies on an electric stovetop, with no fear and no special tools, save a small marble slab and a candy thermometer. I think her true talent was fearlessness.

In 1999, I opened my first chocolate shop, Turtle Alley. Over the years, customers have come in or called with questions about how to make chocolate in their own kitchens. Usually, just a tip here and there proved helpful. I'm happy to have gotten the chance to put this to paper for whomever has the desire to learn a bit and play a bit. It isn't alchemy! As in baking, you just need to know the rules. Once you've got a real feel for the rules, you can start messing around.

This book is broken up into three sections, beginning with the simplest candies and continuing on to the most complicated. The bark section opens with a Master Recipe, and each section that follows adds a Master Recipe to complete each type of recipe. Building your knowledge should build your confidence!

These recipes don't require any special know-how that cannot be

Turtle, Truffle, Bark!

learned from this book. While some candy-making tools are recommended, they aren't absolutely necessary, and none of them cost more than five or ten dollars. Almost all the chocolate-making skills I acquired were first learned through informal lessons, with no fanfare and very little science. This book is about making things in your own damn kitchen that you will love to eat and be proud to share.

In addition to teaching the basics and more, I'd really like to encourage you to follow your own muse when you've got the basics down. Play with flavors. Follow your whimsy with packaging and gift giving. Make a mess. Tell your own story with the ingredients you choose. Write all of your great ideas in the margins. This is the book that wants to be grease-splattered and dog-eared, the one you turn to when you need a lift, or want to get reacquainted with your chocolate dreams.

Barks are as simple as they sound: chocolate spread out on parchment with an offset spatula, to resemble the bark of a tree. Add fruit, nuts, sprinkles, anything you fancy, and you've got it. The secret to a good bark is a good temper on the chocolate when you start. Let's begin with that!

bark

TEMPERING CHOCOLATE

Okay, let's talk about tempering. Simply put, tempering is a process of heating, then cooling chocolate to achieve a beautiful, shiny chocolate that has a nice snap to it when you break it. The simplest method of tempering is known as "seeding." Seeding is basically adding small chunks of unmelted chocolate to melted chocolate.

We'll go light on the science here, but not too light. Tempering, by definition, is the process that helps the cocoa butter in the chocolate to set up into a specific crystalline pattern. Think stacking bricks. If the bricks are well stacked, the structure stays solid. Same thing for chocolate. Get the crystals in the right pattern and the chocolate will achieve the desired results: glossy exterior, smooth mouthfeel, and a nice snap.

Chocolate that isn't tempered can encounter a host of problems: it may not ever set up at room temperature; it may become hard, but have a dull, mottled appearance, the mouthfeel may be crumbly or soggy instead of crisp. Sometimes a "bloom" will happen—this is when the fat solids come to the surface of the chocolate and make whitish splotches or streaks.

Okay. Enough science. Feel free to put all of that information to the back of your mind.

An easy thing to remember when tempering is the old rule, "oil and water don't mix." This is true on a couple of levels: chocolate loves a cool room with little or no humidity, but also, all utensils (and anything that comes in contact with the chocolate) should be completely dry. Water will cause your chocolate to seize during tempering. Seized chocolate will harden into a pasty clump that's impossible to work with. There's no cure for that, except to toss it and try again.

Once you get the hang of it, you probably won't require a thermometer. For novices, however, I highly recommend a chocolate thermometer or a chocolate spatula. Either or can be had for less than ten dollars and will make this process a lot less scary and essentially foolproof. Who doesn't love not scary and foolproof?

So that's a wrap. You've got a little direction and a little science. Now you just need a few tools, tasty chocolate, and a bit of patience. Take a deep breath. This is very doable!

Specialized kitchen utensils and equipment you'll need

Parchment paper

Silicone spatula

Offset spatula

Vinyl gloves

Chef's knife

Medium-sized tempered glass bowl

Chocolate-tempering spatula or chocolate thermometer

*Microwave or double boiler (or a high-sided pan with a
    tempered glass bowl on top of simmering water)*

Option one ♥ microwave method for bark

The general rule of thumb is that you get what you pay for. Premium chocolate with a cocoa percentage of high 60s through mid 70s is recommended. It's strange—I wrote a whole bit about choosing the chocolate you love, as it's an expression of you, and my samples seem to have disappeared . . .

1 pound chocolate

1. Chop chocolate into 1-inch pieces, roughly. Divide chocolate into 3 equal piles.

2. Put two of the piles of chocolate into a glass bowl and put the glass bowl in the microwave.

3. Heat chocolate in the microwave for 30 seconds at a time, mixing often, until chocolate is melted. Be very careful at this stage—chocolate burns very easily. If it burns, it's a total loss.

4. Remove chocolate from microwave and stir gently, scraping sides down to incorporate. Let cool slightly.

5. Add last pile of chocolate into the warm chocolate, stirring briskly with the chocolate spatula, being sure to scrape down the sides, stirring until all chocolate lumps are dissolved.

WHEN IS CHOCOLATE READY?

Milk and white chocolate are tempered at about 88 degrees F. Dark chocolate should be 89–90 degrees F. If you are not using a chocolate-tempering spatula or thermometer, there are a few different ways to gauge the chocolate's readiness: the sides of the bowl will start to feel cool or the chocolate may start to look set on the edges. Dab some chocolate on the inside of your wrist and it should feel cool. A dab on a piece of parchment paper should cool to a glossy finish.

Option two ♥ double boiler method

For turtles and truffles, it's necessary to keep the chocolate tempered for a longer time as you use it. A simple and easy way to do so is by using a heating pad. When you notice the chocolate is becoming thick, simply set it on top of the heating pad on a low setting and stir until it becomes looser and glossy. Be sure not to overheat, or you'll have to temper it all over again!

1 pound chocolate, chopped into 1-inch pieces, divided into thirds

1. Get your double-boiler water simmering, and add ⅔ of the chopped chocolate.

2. Stir with silicone spatula until chocolate is completely melted.

3. Take top pan (or bowl) off double boiler (wiping moisture off the bottom of the bowl), let cool for a minute, and add the last third of chopped chocolate, stirring vigorously until melted and lump free.

4. Stir until seed chocolate is totally melted. Use your chocolate spatula to test temperature. For dark chocolate, it wants to be around 89 to 90 degrees F; for milk or white, around 88. If you don't have a chocolate spatula, spread a little chocolate on parchment paper. In a cool room without humidity, it will start to set up within minutes.

5. For recipes that require the chocolate to stay in temper longer (turtles, chocolate-dipped truffles), when the chocolate gets too cool or seems as though it's getting hard to work with, place it back on top of the double boiler when water has cooled down a bit to be just warm, and stir gently.

PLAIN BARK (MILK, DARK, OR WHITE CHOCOLATE)

This is the one to start with. It concentrates on your tempering method and gets you familiar with the proportions, the tools, and the spreading and cutting of the bark. The best part about this is that if you have trouble with your temper, or spread it too thick or too thin, you can simply retemper your chocolate and start again. At this stage, you can play with how you want to cut your bark and play with toppings. Be adventurous! Plain bark is but a canvas!

What you'll need

2 pounds tempered milk, dark, or white chocolate

1. Lay out a piece of parchment paper on the counter.

2. Pour the tempered chocolate onto the center of the parchment paper, being sure to scrape the sides down with a silicone spatula. Waste nothing!

3. With an offset spatula, lightly spread the chocolate out on the parchment. Keep the thickness uniform (¼ inch to ½ inch thick). Spread chocolate out into a square about 18 × 13 inches.

4. With a gloved hand (you'll thank me later!), lightly drag your fingers through the chocolate in an *S* motion. Let the bark sit until the chocolate has lost its wet look and starts to harden.

5. When it's just set, but not wet looking, cut the bark with a chef's knife. Start the cut with the tip of the knife and rock the rest of the blade into the bark. Remove the knife from the chocolate and continue. If there's too much chocolate buildup on your knife, wash it off, rinsing with cold water. Make sure the knife is completely dry before cutting into the chocolate again.

MILK CHOCOLATE ALMOND BARK

This recipe can, of course, be made with milk, dark, or white chocolate. Although I'm generally a fan of a good, round dark, I do think there's something perfect about what a lovely pair milk chocolate makes with a good roasted, salted almond.

As in all of these recipes, but most of all with these elegant starter recipes, the choice of ingredients is paramount. Finding just the right salted and roasted almond is as crucial as pairing it with your favorite chocolate. Raw almonds are simply not an option in this recipe; they lack the dimension and texture to make a truly satisfying bark.

What you'll need

½ cup roughly chopped roasted, salted almonds

2 pounds tempered milk chocolate

¼ cup chopped almonds to decorate

1. Lay out a piece of parchment paper on the counter.

2. Stir the roasted almonds into the tempered chocolate, incorporating fully.

3. Pour the chocolate and almond mixture onto the center of the parchment paper, being sure to scrape the sides down with a silicone spatula.

4. With your offset spatula, lightly spread the chocolate out on the parchment. Keep the thickness uniform (¼ inch to ½ inch thick). Spread chocolate out into a square about 18 × 13 inches.

5. With a gloved hand, lightly drag your fingers through the chocolate to evenly distribute the almonds. Sprinkle the remaining chopped almonds on the top of the bark.

6. Let the bark sit until the chocolate has lost its wet look and starts to harden.

7. When it's just set, but not wet looking, cut the bark with a chef's knife. Start the cut with the tip of the knife and rock the rest of the blade into the bark. Remove the knife from the chocolate and continue. If there's too much chocolate buildup on the knife, wash it off, rinsing with cold water. Make sure knife is completely dry before cutting into the chocolate again.

8. Stores happily in an airtight container for up to 2 weeks.

MOCHA BARK (MILK OR DARK)

Ah, coffee and chocolate together—a gift from the gods! This one is great in both milk and dark chocolate. If serving with fruit after a meal, I do recommend the deeper flavor of a dark chocolate. Milk chocolate is great if you just want a sweeter treat. The choices you make on extract and coffee beans to grind are crucial here—there are only a few ingredients, so don't skimp!

What you'll need

1 teaspoon coffee extract

2 pounds tempered milk chocolate

¼ cup coarsely ground coffee beans (please grind them yourself— freshly ground beans have a much cleaner flavor)

1. Lay out a piece of parchment paper on the counter.

2. Stir the coffee extract into the chocolate, then the ground coffee.

3. Pour the chocolate mixture onto the center of the parchment paper, being sure to scrape the sides down with a silicone spatula.

4. With an offset spatula, lightly spread the chocolate out on the parchment. Keep the thickness uniform (¼ inch to ½ inch thick). Spread chocolate out into a square about 18 × 13 inches.

5. Let the bark sit until the chocolate has lost its wet look and starts to harden.

6. When it's just set, but not wet looking, cut the bark with a chef's knife. Start the cut with the tip of the knife and rock the rest of the blade into the bark. Remove the knife from the chocolate and continue. If there's too much chocolate buildup on your knife, wash it off, rinsing with cold water. Make sure the knife is completely dry before cutting into the chocolate again.

7. Best for up to 2 weeks, stored in an airtight container.

WHITE CHOCOLATE OREO BARK

This one's pretty, as well as being a tried-and-true favorite with the under-four-foot-tall set. Crush the cookies fairly well, or it may be hard to spread the bark. White chocolate is perfect for this: silky chocolate with the added texture and color of the crushed cookies. You can use any type of cookie you'd like with this one, but I like the look and taste of the classic.

What you'll need

¾ cup crushed Oreos, plus a little extra to sprinkle on top

2 pounds tempered white chocolate

1. Lay out a piece of parchment paper on the counter.

2. Stir the crushed cookies into the tempered chocolate, incorporating fully.

3. Pour the chocolate mixture onto the center of the parchment paper, being sure to scrape the sides down with a silicone spatula.

4. With an offset spatula, lightly spread the chocolate out on the parchment. Keep the thickness uniform (¼ inch to ½ inch thick). Spread chocolate out into a square about 18 × 13 inches.

5. With a gloved hand, lightly drag your fingers through the chocolate to evenly distribute the cookies. Sprinkle the rest of the cookies on the top of the bark if you'd like.

6. Let the bark sit until the chocolate has lost its wet look and starts to harden.

7. When it's just set, but not wet looking, cut the bark with a chef's knife. Start the cut with the tip of the knife and rock the rest of the blade into the bark. Remove the knife from the chocolate and continue. If there's too much chocolate buildup on your knife, wash it off, rinsing with cold water. Make sure knife is completely dry before cutting into the chocolate again.

8. Store for up to 1 week in an airtight container.

MILK CHOCOLATE SESAME DATE BARK

Toasted sesame seeds make all the difference in this simple bark. Besides adding a lovely, nutty note to this bark, it's the perfect playmate for a chopped dried date. Milk chocolate rounds this out to make the balance perfect for this mellow bark. Serve this with tea and lemon, and hold all calls!

What you'll need

¾ cup chopped dried dates

2 pounds tempered milk chocolate

½ cup toasted sesame seeds

1. Lay out a piece of parchment paper on the counter.

2. Stir the chopped dates into the tempered chocolate, incorporating fully.

3. Pour the chocolate mixture onto the center of the parchment paper, being sure to scrape the sides down with a silicone spatula.

4. With an offset spatula, lightly spread the chocolate out on the parchment. Keep the thickness uniform (¼ inch to ½ inch thick). Spread chocolate out into a square about 18×13 inches.

5. With a gloved hand, lightly drag your fingers through the chocolate to evenly distribute the dates. Generously sprinkle the sesame seeds on the top of the bark. (I like to make a real crust with the sesame seeds.)

6. Let the bark sit until the chocolate has lost its wet look and starts to harden.

7. When it's just set, but not wet looking, cut the bark with a chef's knife. Start the cut with the tip of the knife and rock the rest of the blade into the bark. Remove the knife from the chocolate and continue. If there's too much chocolate buildup on your knife, wash it off, rinsing with cold water. Make sure knife is completely dry before cutting into the chocolate again.

8. Store in an airtight container for up to 2 weeks.

TOASTED COCONUT BARK

If you love coconut, this is the bark to try. Milk, dark, or white chocolate works beautifully in this one—it really is about what your preference is. While the title says "toasted," this recipe actually incorporates both toasted and raw coconut. You can use coconut that isn't sweetened, but I really prefer sweetened, long-flake coconut. Aloha!

TOASTED COCONUT

There are a couple of ways to get a nice toasting on coconut: quickly in a microwave, or a little less quickly in an oven.

IN THE MICROWAVE

Spread ½ cup shredded coconut in an even, thin layer on a large microwave-safe plate.

Put in microwave on high for 45 seconds.

Take out and stir, returning to microwave for 30-second increments, stirring each time to prevent burning (that is a horrible smell, by the way), until golden.

IN THE OVEN

Preheat oven to 350 degrees.

Spread ½ cup shredded coconut in an even layer on a sheet pan.

Bake, stirring occasionally, until toasted and golden. Check frequently to avoid burning.

Let coconut fully cool before mixing into chocolate!

What you'll need

½ cup toasted shredded coconut (fully cooled)

¼ cup raw sweetened flake coconut (plus a little more to sprinkle on top)

2 pounds tempered milk chocolate

1. Lay out a piece of parchment paper on the counter.

2. Combine both coconuts and then stir into the tempered chocolate, incorporating fully.

3. Pour the chocolate and coconut mixture onto the center of the parchment paper, being sure to scrape the sides down with a silicone spatula.

4. With an offset spatula, lightly spread the chocolate out on the parchment. Keep the thickness uniform (¼ inch to ½ inch thick). Spread chocolate out into a square about 18×13 inches.

5. With a gloved hand, lightly drag your fingers through the chocolate to evenly distribute the coconut. Sprinkle the remaining raw coconut on top of the bark.

6. Let the bark sit until the chocolate has lost its wet look and starts to harden.

7. When it's just set, but not wet looking, cut the bark with a chef's knife. Start the cut with the tip of the knife and rock the rest of the blade into the bark. Remove the knife from the chocolate and continue. If there's too much chocolate buildup on your knife, wash it off, rinsing with cold water. Make sure knife is completely dry before cutting into the chocolate again.

8. This is happy in an airtight container for up to 2 weeks.

DARK CHOCOLATE MACADAMIA BARK

Salted, roasted macadamia nuts are as rich as it gets in the nut world. We can dial that richness down by pairing the nuts with a good dark chocolate. Macadamias have a sweetness to them that really begs for a not-too-sweet chocolate. Once again, when using just a couple of ingredients, choose the best you can find.

What you'll need

¾ cup roughly chopped roasted, salted macadamia nuts

2 pounds tempered dark chocolate

1. Lay out a piece of parchment paper on the counter.

2. Stir the macadamias into the tempered chocolate, incorporating fully.

3. Pour the chocolate and macadamia mixture onto the center of the parchment paper, being sure to scrape the sides down with a silicone spatula.

4. With an offset spatula, lightly spread the chocolate out on the parchment. Keep the thickness uniform (¼ inch to ½ inch thick). Spread chocolate out into a square about 18×13 inches.

5. With a gloved hand, lightly drag your fingers through the chocolate to evenly distribute the nuts.

6. Let the bark sit until the chocolate has lost its wet look and starts to harden.

7. When it's just set, but not wet looking, cut the bark with a chef's knife. Start the cut with the tip of the knife and rock the rest of the blade into the bark. Remove the knife from the chocolate and continue. If there's too much chocolate buildup on your knife, wash it off, rinsing with cold water. Make sure knife is completely dry before cutting into the chocolate again.

MILK CHOCOLATE PEANUT BUTTER CRISPY BARK

Layer upon layer of childhood memories and guilty pleasures here! Milk chocolate pairs with peanut butter in a most irresistible way, without a doubt. If you're a dark chocolate purist, go right ahead. To my palate, though, the sweetness of the milk chocolate and the saltiness of the peanut butter really complement one another well. To really send this over the top, I stir puffed rice cereal into the bark, then sprinkle with salt. You can make this without the rice cereal, but why would you want to do that?

PEANUT BUTTER ALTERNATIVES

If you want to make this bark for a party, or for your child with a peanut allergy, we have options! My husband and I have been taste-testing peanut butter alternatives for years now (such sacrifice!), and the winner is:

Sunflower seed butter! It has lots of flavor, and the smooth style really has the same mouthfeel as peanut butter.

Almond butter is delicious and will work in this application as well, but the smooth style is a bit lacking in texture.

What you'll need

½ cup scoops peanut butter (see sidebar)

2 pounds tempered milk chocolate

½ cup puffed rice cereal

2 pinches large flake salt

1. Lay out a piece of parchment paper on the counter.

2. Stir the peanut butter into the tempered chocolate, incorporating fully, then fold in the puffed rice cereal.

3. Pour the chocolate mixture onto the center of the parchment paper.

4. With an offset spatula, lightly spread the chocolate out on the parchment. Keep the thickness uniform (¼ inch to ½ inch thick). Spread chocolate out into a square about 18×13 inches.

5. With a gloved hand, lightly drag your fingers through the chocolate to evenly distribute the cereal. Sprinkle the large flake salt lightly across the top of the bark. (Go easy! A little goes a long way.)

6. Let the bark sit until the chocolate has lost its wet look and starts to harden.

7. When it's just set, but not wet looking, cut the bark with a chef's knife. Start the cut with the tip of the knife and rock the rest of the blade into the bark. Remove the knife from the chocolate and continue. If there's too much chocolate buildup on your knife, wash it off, rinsing with cold water. Make sure knife is completely dry before cutting into the chocolate again.

8. Best scarfed up within 2 weeks of storage in an airtight container.

HAZELNUT BARK

Hazelnuts are a love-it-or-hate-it kind of nut, as my experience in the biz has taught me. If you love them, give this recipe a whirl. I adore this in either milk or dark chocolate—it's your call. Toasting the hazelnuts really helps develop the flavor, as does adding a little naughty hazelnut liqueur. I serve this with a big fat red wine, or espresso.

What you'll need

½ cup roughly chopped, toasted hazelnuts (unblanched, if you can find them)

2 pounds tempered milk chocolate

2 tablespoons hazelnut liqueur

1. Lay out a piece of parchment paper on the counter.

2. Stir the hazelnuts into the tempered chocolate, incorporating fully, then add the liqueur. Stir well.

3. Pour the chocolate mixture onto the center of the parchment paper, being sure to scrape the sides down with a silicone spatula.

4. With your offset spatula, lightly spread the chocolate out on the parchment. Keep the thickness uniform (¼ inch to ½ inch thick). Spread chocolate out into a square about 18×13 inches.

5. With a gloved hand, lightly drag your fingers through the chocolate to evenly distribute the hazelnuts. Let the bark sit until the chocolate has lost its wet look and starts to harden.

6. When it's just set, but not wet looking, cut the bark with a chef's knife. Start the cut with the tip of the knife and rock the rest of the blade into the bark. Remove the knife from the chocolate and continue. If there's too much chocolate buildup on your knife, wash it off, rinsing with cold water. Make sure knife is completely dry before cutting into the chocolate again.

7. Stores happily in an airtight container for 2 weeks.

TOAST THOSE NUTS!

Easy, easy peasy!

Heat a heavy skillet over medium heat, toss in nuts, and stir often, until nuts are lightly toasted and fragrant.

This works really well to amplify the flavor of almost any nut, but I wouldn't recommend this treatment with macadamia nuts or cashews. Buy those pre-roasted.

As usual, do make sure your nuts are completely cooled before adding to tempered chocolate.

CRANBERRY ORANGE BARK

This bark reminds me of the holidays and all the sweets and savories studded with fruit. It's a lovely gift that's easy to make, and frankly, it feels pretty good to be able to give something you've made and packed yourself. It's not a bad idea to scour the shelves in the off-season to find cool and unique tins or jars in which to present this bark. My strong opinion is that this bark truly shines when made with dark chocolate.

What you'll need

1 teaspoon orange extract, tossed with ¼ cup chopped, candied orange peel

2 pounds tempered dark chocolate

½–¾ cup chopped, dried cranberries, divided

1. Lay out a piece of parchment paper on the counter.

2. Stir the orange extract and peel into the chocolate, then the cranberries, reserving a third of the cranberries to sprinkle on top at the end. They can look jewel-like, and really add to the festivity of the bark.

3. Pour the chocolate in the center of the parchment paper. Scrape the sides down and start spreading the chocolate out to a uniform thickness with the offset spatula. Work fast—when you add several ingredients, it tends to set up a bit faster than plain chocolate. Get your fingers in there, too, to spread out the cranberries and orange peel the best you can. Spread to approximately 18×13 inches. Sprinkle reserved cranberries on top.

4. Let the bark sit until the chocolate has lost its wet look and starts to harden.

5. When it's just set, but not moist, cut the bark with a chef's knife. Start the cut with the tip of the knife and rock the rest of the blade into the bark. Make sure you are completely cutting through the fruit so the finished pieces of bark are easy to separate.

6. Store in an airtight container for up to 3 weeks.

GUMMI BARK

This has children's birthday party written all over it. Creamy chocolate studded with gummi candies—fish, bears, worms, frogs, you name it! Go with one type of gummi, or bring the whole zoo! The wee ones seem to like a sweeter chocolate in general, so choose between milk or white. Sophisticates can do their dark chocolate thing.

What you'll need

2 pounds tempered milk or white chocolate

1 cup gummi candy—the more, the merrier!

1. Lay out a piece of parchment paper on the counter.

2. Pour the chocolate onto the center of the parchment paper, being sure to scrape the sides down with a silicone spatula.

3. With an offset spatula, lightly spread the chocolate out on the parchment. Keep the thickness uniform (about ½ inch thick). Spread chocolate out into a square about 16×11 inches.

4. Generously sprinkle gummi candy all over this bark. Overkill is encouraged!

5. Let the bark sit until the chocolate has lost its wet look and starts to harden.

6. When it's just set, but not wet looking, cut the bark with a chef's knife. Start the cut with the tip of the knife and rock the rest of the blade into the bark. Remove the knife from the chocolate and continue. If there's too much chocolate buildup on your knife, wash it off, rinsing with cold water. Make sure knife is completely dry before cutting into the chocolate again.

7. Store in an airtight container up to 3 weeks.

ROCKY ROAD BARK

While it is always an option to use any color of chocolate you like in this recipe, my sense is that the folks who will go wild for this tried-and-true combination will prefer milk chocolate. Bring on the guilty pleasures!

Two things will set this apart from other Rocky Road fare: a light toasting of the walnuts, and using mini marshmallows, inside and out. The marshmallows that get cut in half may dry a bit, but we'll stud the top of the bark with whole ones, so there will be squishy ones too!

TOASTING WALNUTS

This is simply done. Just heat a heavy skillet over medium heat, throw the walnuts in, and toss until they get slightly brown and give off a beautiful walnutty aroma. Heaven! Let them cool completely before giving them a coarse chop.

What you'll need

⅓ cup toasted walnuts

½ cup small marshmallows, plus extra to sprinkle on top

2 pounds tempered milk chocolate

1. Lay out a piece of parchment paper on the counter.

2. Stir walnuts and marshmallows into the tempered chocolate with the silicone spatula. Fold gently until fully incorporated.

3. Pour the mixture onto the center of the parchment paper, being sure to scrape the sides down with the silicone spatula.

4. With an offset spatula, lightly spread the chocolate out on the parchment. Keep the thickness uniform (¼ inch to ½ inch thick). Spread chocolate out into a square about 18×12 inches.

5. With a gloved hand, lightly drag your fingers through the chocolate to evenly distribute the marshmallows. Place extra marshmallows on top of bark, just about every inch.

6. Let the bark sit until the chocolate has lost its wet look and starts to harden.

7. When it's just set, but not wet looking, cut the bark with a chef's knife. Start the cut with the tip of the knife and rock the rest of the blade into the bark. Do your best not to cut the marshmallows on top, as we don't want them to get too dried out. Remove the knife from the chocolate and continue. If there's too much chocolate (or marshmallow) buildup on your knife, wash it off, rinsing with cold water. Make sure knife is completely dry before cutting into the chocolate again.

8. This bark is happy to be stored in an airtight container (to keep the marshmallows as soft as possible), with parchment in between layers, at room temperature, for a week. Make sure the seal is tight. Or, do as I do: make this the day it's going to be consumed. I guarantee there will be no leftovers!

PRETZEL BARK

Pretzels with chocolate isn't just for the ladies. Salty, crunchy, sweet? Yes, please! Go with the small pretzel knot shape. We're going to place these on top of the wet chocolate and then cut around them. Milk, dark, or white—choose your chocolatey poison!

What you'll need

2 pounds tempered chocolate

50–60 small pretzels

1. Lay out a piece of parchment paper on the counter.

2. Pour the chocolate onto the center of the parchment paper, being sure to scrape the sides down with a silicone spatula.

3. With an offset spatula, lightly spread the chocolate out on the parchment. Keep the thickness uniform (¼ inch to ½ inch thick). Spread chocolate out into a square about 18×13 inches.

4. When the chocolate is just starting to firm up, but not hard, set a pretzel into the chocolate about every 2 inches left to right, 1 ½ to 2 inches apart top to bottom (approximately 9 across, 6 or 7 top to bottom).

5. When it's just set, but not wet looking, cut the bark with a chef's knife (be sure not to cut through pretzels). Start the cut with the tip of the knife and rock the rest of the blade into the bark. Remove the knife from the chocolate and continue. If there's too much chocolate buildup on your knife, wash it off, rinsing with cold water. Make sure knife is completely dry before cutting into the chocolate again.

6. These are good stored in an airtight container for about 1 week.

KITCHEN SINK BARK

Wondering what to do with those bits and bobs left over from baking projects? Have some nuts and dried fruits you'd like to cycle out of your pantry? Just feel like messing around with flavor and texture? This is just what it sounds like: combine whatever you have that you'd like to get rid of, and mix into milk, dark, or white chocolate. Let your imagination run wild! Have no fear—if it's mixed into chocolate, it will get eaten.*

    *Hold the sardines.

What you'll need

½–¾ cup of your personal kitchen sink mix (¾ cup will make it really chunky, but what the heck, this is about recycling!)

2 pounds tempered milk chocolate

1. Lay out a piece of parchment paper on the counter.

2. Stir the kitchen sink mix into the tempered chocolate, incorporating fully.

3. Pour the chocolate mixture onto the center of the parchment paper, being sure to scrape the sides down with a silicone spatula.

4. With your offset spatula, lightly spread the chocolate out on the parchment. Keep the thickness uniform (¼ inch to ½ inch thick). Spread chocolate out into a square about 18×13 inches.

5. With a gloved hand, lightly drag your fingers through the chocolate to evenly distribute the mix.

6. Let the bark sit until the chocolate has lost its wet look and starts to harden.

7. When it's just set, but not wet looking, cut the bark with a chef's knife. Start the cut with the tip of the knife and rock the rest of the blade into the bark. Remove the knife from the chocolate and continue. If there's too much chocolate buildup on your knife, wash it off, rinsing with cold water. Make sure knife is completely dry before cutting into the chocolate.

8. Stores happily in an airtight container for 2 weeks.

WHITE CHOCOLATE CASHEW BARK WITH CRANBERRIES

Any time I make a bark with white chocolate, I'm always delighted with how the mellow ivory color of the chocolate looks with whatever I've decided to mix in. This one goes heavy on the rich and smooth, but has a bit of tart sprinkled on top at the last minute. The cranberries add a much-needed element to brighten up the creaminess of the cashews and the white chocolate.

What you'll need

1/2 cup roughly chopped roasted, salted cashews

2 pounds tempered white chocolate

1/2 cup dried cranberries

1. Lay out a piece of parchment paper on the counter.

2. Stir the cashews into the tempered chocolate, incorporating fully.

3. Pour the chocolate mixture onto the center of the parchment paper, being sure to scrape the sides down with a silicone spatula.

4. With your offset spatula, lightly spread the chocolate out on the parchment. Keep the thickness uniform (1/4 inch to 1/2 inch thick). Spread chocolate out into a square about 8×13 inches.

5. With a gloved hand, lightly drag your fingers through the chocolate to evenly distribute the cashews. Sprinkle the cranberries on the top of the bark.

6. Let the bark sit until the chocolate has lost its wet look and starts to harden.

7. When it's just set, but not wet looking, cut the bark with a chef's knife. Start the cut with the tip of the knife and rock the rest of the blade into the bark. Remove the knife from the chocolate and continue. If there's too much chocolate buildup on your knife, wash it off, rinsing with cold water. Make sure knife is completely dry before cutting into the chocolate again.

8. Store in an airtight container for up to 2 weeks.

DARK CHOCOLATE MOCHA CHERRY BARK

Here we get to play with flavor and texture. This sort of flavor combination is really what makes my heart sing. Sound a little wacky? Maybe too much going on? Perfect!

As a general rule of thumb, my opinion about fruit and chocolate is that the chocolate should be dark. To my palate, milk chocolate falls flat when paired with a deep tart cherry or a bright citrus note.

If you change all my other dark recipes to milk or white chocolate, please do me the favor of trying this one first in dark. Trust me. I'm a professional!

What you'll need

1 teaspoon coffee extract

¼ teaspoon almond extract (secret weapon! Tell no one!)

2 pounds tempered dark chocolate

½–¾ cup chopped dried tart cherries

1. Lay out a piece of parchment paper on the counter.

2. Stir the coffee and almond extracts into the chocolate, then the cherries.

3. Pour the chocolate in the center of the parchment paper. Scrape the sides down and start spreading the chocolate out to a uniform thickness with the offset spatula. Work fast—when you add ingredients to a bark, it tends to set up fast. Use your gloved fingers to spread out the cherries if they get bunched up. Spread to about 18×13 inches.

4. Let the bark sit until the chocolate has lost its wet look and starts to harden.

5. When it's just set, but not moist, cut the bark with a chef's knife. Start the cut with the tip of the knife and rock the rest of the blade into the bark. Make sure you are completely cutting through the cherries so the finished pieces of bark are easy to separate. I love to make a diamond pattern when cutting this one; it lets those garnet-like dried cherries really shine.

6. This bark should be stored in an airtight container, layered with parchment paper. The extracts can lose potency if they hang out in open air too long, so make sure to box or jar it up when you're done taste-testing.

7. FYI: This bark is outstanding chopped up and sprinkled on ice cream, or used in any cookie recipe!

DARK AND WHITE PEPPERMINT BARK

A holiday favorite, this bark is tradition and treat all in one! While it isn't necessary to top with crushed candy canes, you know you'll want to.

Note: this recipe is a bit more advanced, so get some successful tempering under your belt before you attempt it!

What you'll need

1/2 teaspoon peppermint oil

1 pound tempered dark chocolate

1 pound tempered white chocolate

3/4 cup crushed candy canes

1. Stir the peppermint oil into the dark chocolate, then spread the dark chocolate in a thin layer (1/4 inch) onto parchment paper. Spread to make about a 12×10-inch square. Be sure to keep thickness as even as you can. Let sit for a few minutes until it just starts to set, but is not hard. If white chocolate seems to be getting cool, put the bowl on a heating pad set to low, and stir it until it loosens up.

2. Before the dark chocolate gets hard (it needs to be slightly wet for the white chocolate to stick to it), carefully spread the white chocolate on top of the dark. Use a light hand so you are actually spreading on top, not mixing the two chocolates together.

3. Sprinkle crushed candy canes on top. I like to really crust it over with the candy canes, but please do as you see fit. This is your bark!

4. When it's just set, but not wet looking, cut the bark with a chef's knife. Start the cut with the tip of the knife and rock the rest of the blade into the bark. Remove the knife from the chocolate and continue. If there's too much chocolate buildup on your knife, wash it off, rinsing with cold water. Make sure knife is completely dry before cutting into the chocolate again.

5. In a festive tin, this makes a perfect holiday gift. For best results, bag up in cellophane, then put in tins.

Behold, the holy trinity of candy!
Chocolate, nuts, and caramel make
this beauty what it is. You've already
learned how to temper chocolate,
so we'll start with a Master Recipe
for a most essential element of a
tasty turtle: caramel.

turtles

CARAMEL

For this master recipe, I'm going to give you two options: the first will be as simple as they come, in which you purchase premade caramel and melt it to make your turtle middles. There's a lot of really beautiful caramel out there, so don't scoff! It makes sense to start the turtle process simply, and in this case, that means buying your caramel. That way, you can concentrate on your chocolate tempering without having to sweat making your own caramel as well.

If you've got tempering down, or feel like you want to take it all on, the second option is for you. Option number two is a simple recipe for caramel—not too many ingredients, not too much of a time investment. Tastes lovely and looks beautiful, too.

Specialized kitchen utensils and equipment you'll need

18×13-inch sheet pan (some recipes require 2 pans)

Parchment paper

Medium-sized tempered glass bowl (or heavy-bottomed saucepan)

Microwave (or stovetop)

Silicone spatulas, one medium sized, one small

Candy funnel

If making your own caramel from scratch, you'll also need

Heavy-bottomed saucepan

A standard (2-ounce) ice cream scoop

A cup with cold water in it, deep enough to cover the scoop

Candy thermometer

Option one ♥ premade caramel

4–6 cups nuts, according to recipe

¾ pound caramel

1 pat butter (for stovetop method)

1. Line a sheet pan with parchment paper. Spread nuts in an even layer on the parchment. Set aside.

2. Place caramel into bowl. Put bowl in microwave, and heat on high for 45 seconds to 1 minute.

3. Take out of microwave, stir well with medium-sized spatula, put back in for 30 seconds.

4. At this point, your caramel should be in liquid form. A little firmer is okay!

5. Stovetop option: Lightly coat inside of saucepan with a pat of butter (to prevent sticking). Add caramel. Stir over low heat until it is in liquid form. If it feels as though it's getting stiff, you can add a little water (a teaspoon at a time) to loosen it until it is liquid.

6. Scoop a dollop of caramel from the bowl or saucepan with your small silicone spatula, and using your other spatula, ease the caramel off the spatula and onto the nuts. You've made a turtle middle! The size should be from 1 ½ to 2 inches in diameter, depending on the size of the turtles you'd like to make.

7. Continue in this manner until all the melted caramel is used. You will have about 20 to 25 middles. When caramel is completely cooled, you can start assembling your turtles. Any extra nuts on the tray will serve as well-deserved sustenance for you and any helpers you might have!

Option two ❤ homemade caramel

Some recipes just don't like to be halved. This is one of them! Note that this batch size will make two trays of turtle middles, not one. You can store half of the batch in an airtight container (for up to 2 to 3 weeks) for a later project, if you'd rather make one tray of turtles at a time.

4–6 cups nuts per tray, according to recipe

1¼ cups white sugar

3 tablespoons salted butter

10 ounces corn syrup (5 2-ounce scoops)

5 ounces heavy cream

1½ cups evaporated milk

½ teaspoon salt, or more, to taste

1. Line two sheet pans with parchment paper. Spread nuts in an even layer on the parchment. Set aside.

2. Place ice cream scoop in cup of cold water, and set aside.

3. Combine sugar, butter, corn syrup, and heavy cream in a heavy-bottomed saucepan, using a 2-ounce ice cream scoop to measure corn syrup. Over medium heat, bring to a boil, stirring gently. Place a candy thermometer into the caramel. Let it boil until it reaches 225 degrees F.

4. Add evaporated milk and stir well. At this point, the caramel will rise in the pan. Let it boil until it reduces by about half its volume. As it reduces, be sure to stir regularly, and scrape the bottom of the pan to prevent scorching. Cook until the temperature reads 230 degrees F.

5. Remove from heat.

6. Add ½ teaspoon salt. (You can add more to taste when you are assembling your turtles.) Stir gently to incorporate.

7. At this point, you can continue on as you would in the last part of option one, or you can put the caramel in an airtight container to store for the future. Don't cover it until the caramel has completely cooled! It'll last up to 2 weeks at room temperature. To get it to liquid consistency when ready to use, zap it in the microwave for 30 seconds at a time on high until it's liquid. No boiling on the second heat up!

TIPS FOR TURTLE ASSEMBLY!

Turtles are basically a chocolate, nut, and caramel sandwich. While the caramel recipe tells you how to make a turtle middle, this little sidebar is going to help you with the actual turtle construction. Tips and tools are your friends!

First, go ahead and spend four or five dollars on a small, plastic candy funnel. The ones that hold about 1 to 1¼ cups of chocolate are ideal. You will thank me for this later. In a pinch, you can use a pair of spoons for the chocolate part of a turtle, but it might break your heart. I tried it, and it nearly broke mine.

Second, make sure your caramel is totally cool to the touch before assembly. Even slightly warm caramel will throw off the temper of the chocolate, and you know you don't want to do that!

Last, take your time, and enjoy the process. Chocolates made with love always taste better! Don't be nervous, and don't be afraid of a little mess here and there.

P.S. Chocolate on your shirt? Let it harden, flake it off, then spray it with window cleaner. No, really! It works!

TURTLE ASSEMBLY

1–2 pounds tempered chocolate (depending on the size batch of caramel you've decided upon)

20–24 (or 40–48, depending on batch size) caramel turtle middles

1. Using a candy funnel, deposit dollops of chocolate on the parchment paper. Each one should be approximately 1½ inches in diameter, and there should be about an inch between each dollop. Make about six dollops, and then place a caramel middle on top of each one. Continue making bottoms, topping with caramel, every six or so. When you have got all your bottoms and middles done, go back to where you started and top the caramel with chocolate. Use enough chocolate to mostly cover the caramel, then finish with a swirl. Turtles can now be decorated any which way!

2. When turtles are completely hardened, they will keep in an airtight container for 3 weeks, but they never last that long!

MILK CHOCOLATE PECAN TURTLES

We'll start the turtle section of the book with one of the most popular turtles on the planet, the pecan turtle. Pecan turtles are the traditional favorite and are simple and satisfying when the pecans are of top quality. Make sure your nuts are fresh! Most pecans are raw, and can lose their freshness quickly, so perform a much-needed quality control test before assembly (oh, the horror!). The hands-down favorite of the masses on this turtle is milk chocolate, but I really think they are tasty in any color. You choose.

To simplify this first turtle recipe, let's use premade caramel. As we get rolling in this chapter, you can splash out and make your own.

What you'll need

4 cups pecans

¾ pound caramel

1 pound tempered milk chocolate

1. Line a sheet pan with parchment paper. Spread pecans in an even layer on the parchment. Set aside.

2. Place caramel into a bowl, and microwave on high for 45 seconds to 1 minute.

3. Take out of microwave, stir well with medium-sized spatula, and put back in for 30 seconds.

4. At this point, your caramel should be in liquid form. A little firmer is okay!

5. Scoop a dollop of caramel from the bowl with your small silicone spatula, and using your other spatula, ease the caramel off the spatula and onto the nuts. Try to make the caramel about 1 ½ inch to 2 inches in diameter, depending on the size of the turtles you'd like to make. You'll end up with 20 to 24 caramel middles.

TURTLE ASSEMBLY

1. Line an 18×13-inch baking pan with parchment paper. Using a candy funnel, deposit dollops of chocolate on the parchment paper. Each one should be approximately 1 ½ inches in diameter, and there should be about an inch between each dollop. Make about six dollops, and then place a caramel middle on top of each one. Continue making bottoms, topping with caramel, every six or so. When you have got all your bottoms and middles done, go back to where you started and top the caramel with chocolate. Use enough chocolate to mostly cover the caramel, then finish with a swirl.

2. When turtles are completely hardened, they will last in an airtight container for 3 weeks.

DARK CASHEW TURTLES

This was my very first favorite turtle. Even now, when I need a little something from the turtle world, this one completely satisfies me. Cashews can be such a sweet, rich nut—I think dark chocolate is just the thing for this recipe. Trust me. Be sure to use roasted, salted cashews.

In keeping with "simple starts the chapter," let's use premade caramel again.

What you'll need

5 cups cashews, plus extra for decoration

¾ pound caramel

1 pound tempered dark chocolate

1. Line a sheet pan with parchment paper. Spread nuts in an even layer on the parchment. Set aside.

2. Place prepared caramel into bowl. Microwave on high for 45 seconds to 1 minute.

3. Take out of microwave, stir well with medium-sized spatula, put back in for 30 seconds.

4. At this point, your caramel should be in liquid form. A little firmer is okay!

5. Scoop a dollop of caramel from the bowl with your small silicone spatula, and using your other spatula, ease the caramel off the spatula and onto the nuts. Try to make the caramel about 1½ inch to 2 inches in diameter, depending on the size of the turtles you'd like to make. You'll end up with twenty to twenty-four caramel middles.

TURTLE ASSEMBLY

1. Line an 18×13-inch baking pan with parchment paper. Using a candy funnel, deposit dollops of chocolate on the parchment paper. Each one should be approximately 1½ inches in diameter, and there should be about an inch between each dollop. Make about six dollops, and then place a caramel middle on top of each one. Continue making bottoms, topping with caramel, every six or so. When you have got all your bottoms and middles done, go back to where you started and top the caramel with chocolate. You want to use enough chocolate to mostly cover the caramel. Top each turtle with a perfect curlicue of a cashew.

2. When turtles are completely hardened, they will last in an airtight container for 2 weeks.

WHITE CHOCOLATE ALMOND TURTLES

Oh, the decadence! White chocolate turtles are perhaps the most luxurious of the bunch, with their tremendously smooth and silky mouthfeel. I like to make white turtles with almonds; the almonds really showcase the silkiness of the white chocolate without sending them too far over the sweet edge. The added crunch of a roasted almond plays perfectly against all that smooth silkiness! At the end, top with just a touch of large flake salt. Don't mind if I do!

After you've got these under your belt, the sky's the limit!

What you'll need

5 cups roasted, salted almonds

¾ pound caramel

1 pound tempered white chocolate

Large flake salt, for decorating

1. Line a sheet pan with parchment paper. Spread nuts in an even layer on the parchment. Set aside.

2. Place caramel into bowl. Microwave on high for 45 seconds to 1 minute. Take out of microwave, stir well with medium-sized spatula, and put back in for 30 seconds. At this point, your caramel should be in liquid form. A little firmer is okay!

3. Scoop a dollop of caramel from the bowl with your small silicone spatula, and using your other spatula, ease the caramel off the spatula and onto the nuts. Try to make the caramel about 1½ to 2 inches in diameter, depending on the size of the turtles you'd like to make. You'll end up with 20 to 24 caramel middles.

TURTLE ASSEMBLY

1. Line an 18×13-inch baking pan with parchment paper. Using a candy funnel, deposit dollops of chocolate on the parchment paper. Each one should be approximately 1½ inches in diameter, and there should be about an inch between each dollop. Make about six dollops, and then place a caramel middle on top of each one. Continue making bottoms, topping with caramel, every six or so. When you have got all your bottoms and middles done, go back to where you started and top the caramel with chocolate. Use enough chocolate to mostly cover the caramel, then finish with a swirl.

2. Top with just a touch of large flake salt.

3. When turtles are completely hardened, they will last in an airtight container for 3 weeks.

MILK CHOCOLATE CHUNKY TURTLES

One of my mother's favorite candies during my childhood inspired this turtle. The combination of peanuts, milk chocolate, and raisins might seem a bit much at first, but trust me, these turtles are addictive! Be sure to buy the plumpest raisins you can find and that your peanuts are salted. This one is really good in milk chocolate. I like to top these off with whatever fun sprinkle I can find; these turtles just seem playful to me. Ah, childhood . . .

Option one ♥ premade caramel

4 cups peanuts

2 cups raisins

¾ pound purchased caramel

1 pound tempered milk chocolate

Fun sprinkles to finish (optional)

1. Line a sheet pan with parchment paper. Spread peanuts in an even layer on the parchment. Sprinkle raisins on top of peanuts. Set aside.

2. Place prepared caramel into bowl. Put bowl in microwave, and heat on high for 45 seconds to 1 minute. Take out of microwave, stir well with medium-sized spatula, put back in for 30 seconds.

3. At this point, your caramel should be in liquid form. A little firmer is okay!

4. Scoop a dollop of caramel from the bowl with your small silicone spatula, and using your other spatula, ease the caramel off the spatula and onto the nuts. Try to make them anywhere from 1½ to 2 inches in diameter, depending on the size of the turtles you'd like to make. You'll end up with 20 to 24 caramel middles.

5. When caramel is completely cooled, you can start assembling your turtles (see page 68).

Option two ♥ homemade caramel

Some recipes just don't like to be halved. This is one of them! Note that this batch size will make two trays of turtle middles, not one. You may always store half of the batch in an airtight container for a later project if you don't want to do a whole batch at one time.

4 cups peanuts per tray

2 cups raisins per tray

1 ¼ cups white sugar

3 tablespoons salted butter

10 ounces corn syrup (5 2-ounce scoops)

5 ounces heavy cream

1 ½ cups evaporated milk

½ teaspoon salt, or more, to taste

1–2 pounds tempered milk chocolate, depending on the size batch of caramel you've decided on

Fun sprinkles to finish (optional)

1. Line sheet pans with parchment paper. Spread peanuts in an even layer on the parchment. Sprinkle raisins on top of peanuts. Set aside.

2. Place ice cream scoop in cup of cold water, and set aside.

3. Combine sugar, butter, corn syrup, and heavy cream in a heavy-bottomed saucepan, using the ice cream scoop to measure corn syrup. Over medium heat, bring to a boil, stirring gently. Place a candy thermometer into the caramel. Let it boil until it reaches 225 degrees F.

4. Add evaporated milk and stir well. At this point, the caramel will rise in the pan. Let it boil until it reduces by about half its volume. As it reduces, be sure to stir regularly, and scrape the bottom of the pan to prevent scorching. Cook until the temperature reads 230 degrees F.

5. Remove from heat.

6. Add salt (I'd start with ½ teaspoon. You can always add more when you are assembling your turtles) and stir gently to incorporate.

continued ...

7. At this point, you can continue on as you would in the last part of option one to form the turtle middles. You'll end up with 20 to 24 or 44 to 48 caramel middles, depending on the batch size you're making. Remember, if you choose to just use half the batch, you can put the rest in an airtight container to store for the future. Be sure not to cover it until the caramel has completely cooled. It'll last up to 2 weeks at room temperature. To get it to liquid consistency if you are storing it for later, use 30-second, high-setting zaps in the microwave until it is liquid. Don't let it get to boiling, or it will turn very hard and chewy. You've been warned!

TURTLE ASSEMBLY

1. Line one or two 18×13-inch sheet pans with parchment paper, depending on the size batch of caramel you've decided on. Using your candy funnel, deposit dollops of chocolate on the parchment paper. Each one should be approximately 1½ inches in diameter, and there should be about an inch between each dollop. Make about six dollops, and then place a caramel middle on top of each one. Continue making bottoms, topping with caramel, every six or so. When you have got all your bottoms and middles done, go back to where you started and top the caramel with chocolate. You want to use enough chocolate to mostly cover the caramel, then finish with a swirl or fun sprinkles.

2. When turtles are completely hardened, they will last in an airtight container for 3 weeks.

MAPLE WALNUT TURTLES

Maple and walnut are a classic combination of flavors that can please a crowd anytime, anywhere. Milk chocolate is my recommendation for these—it complements the maple without overpowering it, as well as showcasing the comfort-food feel.

We're going to make our own candied maple walnuts, so premade caramel works just swell in this recipe.

What you'll need

5 cups maple walnuts (see sidebar)

¾ pound caramel

1 pound tempered milk chocolate

1. Line a sheet pan with parchment paper. Spread walnuts in an even layer on the parchment. Set aside.

2. Place prepared caramel into bowl. Put bowl in microwave, and heat on high for 45 seconds to 1 minute. Take out of microwave, stir well with medium-sized spatula, and put back in for 30 seconds. At this point, your caramel should be in liquid form. A little firmer is okay!

3. Scoop a dollop of caramel from the bowl with your small silicone spatula, and using your other spatula, ease the caramel off the spatula and onto the nuts. Try to make them anywhere from 1½ to 2 inches in diameter, depending on the size of the turtles you'd like to make. You'll end up with 20 to 24 turtle middles.

4. When caramel is completely cooled, you can start assembling your turtles.

TURTLE ASSEMBLY

1. Line an 18×13-inch sheet pan with parchment paper. Using a candy funnel, deposit dollops of chocolate on the parchment paper. Each one should be approximately 1 ½ inches in diameter, and there should be about an inch between each dollop. Make about six dollops, and then place a caramel middle on top of each one. Continue making bottoms, topping with caramel, every six or so. When you have got all your bottoms and middles done, go back to where you started and top the caramel with chocolate. You want to use enough chocolate to mostly cover the caramel, then top it with a walnut or a swirl.

2. When turtles are completely hardened, they will last in an airtight container for 1 week, tops.

MAPLE WALNUTS

5 cups walnuts
¾ cup maple syrup
½ teaspoon salt

Line an 18×13-inch sheet pan with parchment paper.

Toast the nuts in a dry, heavy-bottomed saucepan large enough to hold all the nuts (or make this recipe in two batches, if your pan is too small), tossing to distribute heat evenly. Toast until fragrant.

Add maple syrup and salt, stirring all the while to prevent burning.

Cook until syrup is crystallized, and pour out onto sheet pan.

Let cool completely before making your turtle middles.

DARK CHOCOLATE PISTACHIO TURTLES

Pistachios are one of those nuts that are dangerous to have around the house. Once that bag is open, it's over. Paired with dark chocolate, these turtles have a strong but simple flavor set. The pistachios should be roasted and salted. These are best eaten within days, as pistachios get soft over time. I guarantee you won't have any trouble getting rid of them!

Option one ♥ premade caramel

5 cups shelled, roasted, salted pistachios

¾ pound purchased caramel

1 pound tempered dark chocolate

1. Line a sheet pan with parchment paper. Spread pistachios in an even layer on the parchment. Set aside.

2. Place prepared caramel into bowl. Put bowl in microwave, and heat on high for 45 seconds to 1 minute. Take out of microwave, stir well with medium-sized spatula, and put back in for 30 seconds. At this point, your caramel should be in liquid form. A little firmer is okay!

3. Scoop a dollop of caramel from the bowl with a small silicone spatula, and using another spatula, ease the caramel off the spatula and onto the nuts. Try to make them anywhere from 1½ to 2 inches in diameter, depending on the size of the turtles you'd like to make. You'll end up with 20 to 24 caramel middles.

4. When caramel is completely cooled, you can start assembling your turtles (see next page).

Option two ❤ homemade caramel

Note that this batch size will make two trays of turtle middles, not one. You may always store half of the batch in an airtight container for a later project if you don't want to do a whole batch at one time.

> 5 cups shelled, roasted, salted pistachios per tray
>
> 1¼ cups white sugar
>
> 3 tablespoons salted butter
>
> 10 ounces corn syrup (5 2-ounce scoops)
>
> 5 ounces heavy cream
>
> 1½ cups evaporated milk
>
> ½ teaspoon salt, or more, to taste
>
> 1–2 pounds tempered dark chocolate, depending on the size batch of caramel you've decided on

1. Line two sheet pans with parchment paper. Spread pistachios in an even layer on the parchment. Set aside.

2. Place ice cream scoop in cup of cold water, and set aside.

3. Combine sugar, butter, corn syrup, and heavy cream in a heavy-bottomed saucepan, using the ice cream scoop to measure corn syrup. Over medium heat, bring to a boil, stirring gently. Place a candy thermometer into the caramel. Let it boil until it reaches 225 degrees F.

4. Add evaporated milk and stir well. At this point, the caramel will rise in the pan. Let it boil until it reduces by about half its volume. As it reduces, be sure to stir regularly, and scrape the bottom of the pan to prevent scorching. Cook until the temperature reads 230 degrees F.

5. Remove from heat.

6. Add salt. (You can add more to taste when you are assembling your turtles.) Stir gently to incorporate.

7. At this point, you can continue on as you would in the last part of option one to form the turtle middles. You'll have 20 to 24 caramel turtle middles, or 40 to 48, depending on the batch size you're making. Remember, if you choose to just use half the batch, you can put the rest in an airtight container to store for the future. Be sure not to cover it until the caramel has completely cooled. It'll last up to 2 weeks at room temperature. To get it to liquid consistency if you are storing it for later, use 30-second, high-setting zaps in the microwave until it is liquid. Don't let it get to boiling, or it will turn very hard and chewy. You've been warned!

TURTLE ASSEMBLY

1. Using your candy funnel, deposit dollops of chocolate on one or two 18×24-inch baking sheets lined with parchment paper. Each one should be approximately 1½ inches in diameter, and there should be about an inch between each dollop. Make about six dollops, and then place a caramel middle on top of each one. Continue making bottoms, topping with caramel, every six or so. When you have got all your bottoms and middles done, go back to where you started and top the caramel with chocolate. You want to use enough chocolate to mostly cover the caramel, then finish with a swirl.

2. When turtles are completely hardened, they will last in an airtight container for 1 week, tops.

BLACK-AND-WHITE TURTLES

In this recipe, we put together a deep, dark macadamia turtle and drizzle white chocolate over the top. Macadamias are sweet nuts that like to be paired with a serious dark chocolate. The white chocolate drizzle looks lovely without upsetting the play of flavor between the dark chocolate and the macadamias. Serve these for dessert with a ruby red port and say good night, Gracie!

Option one ♥ premade caramel

5 cups macadamia nuts (salted or unsalted, what's your pleasure?)

¾ pound caramel

1 pound tempered dark chocolate

½ pound tempered white chocolate

1. Line a sheet pan with parchment paper. Spread macadamias in an even layer on the parchment. Set aside.

2. Place prepared caramel into a bowl. Put bowl in microwave, and heat on high for 45 seconds to 1 minute. Take out of microwave, stir well with medium-sized spatula, and put back in for 30 seconds. At this point, your caramel should be in liquid form. A little firmer is okay!

3. Scoop a dollop of caramel from the bowl with your small silicone spatula, and using your other spatula, ease the caramel off the spatula and onto the nuts. Try to make them anywhere from 1½ to 2 inches in diameter, depending on the size of the turtles you'd like to make.

4. When caramel is completely cooled, you can start assembling your turtles (see next page).

Option two ❤ homemade caramel

This batch size will make two trays of turtle middles, not one. You can store half of the batch in an airtight container for a later project if you don't want to do a whole batch at one time.

> 5 cups macadamia nuts per tray (salted or unsalted)
>
> 1 ¼ cups white sugar
>
> 3 tablespoons salted butter
>
> 10 ounces corn syrup (5 2-ounce scoops)
>
> 5 ounces heavy cream
>
> 1 ½ cups evaporated milk
>
> ½ teaspoon salt, or more, to taste
>
> 1–2 pounds tempered dark chocolate, depending on the size batch of caramel you've decided on
>
> ½ pound–¾ pound tempered white chocolate

1. Line two sheet pans with parchment paper. Spread macadamias in an even layer on the parchment. Set aside.

2. Place ice cream scoop in cup of cold water, and set aside.

3. Combine sugar, butter, corn syrup, and heavy cream in a heavy-bottomed saucepan, using the ice cream scoop to measure corn syrup. Over medium heat, bring to a boil, stirring gently. Place a candy thermometer into the caramel. Let it boil until it reaches 225 degrees F.

4. Add evaporated milk and stir well. At this point, the caramel will rise in the pan. Let it boil until it reduces by about half its volume. As it reduces, be sure to stir regularly, and scrape the bottom of the pan to prevent scorching. Cook until the temperature reads 230 degrees F.

5. Remove from heat.

6. Add salt. (You can add more to taste when you are assembling your turtles.) Stir gently to incorporate.

7. At this point, you can continue on as you would in the last part of option one to form the turtle middles. You'll end up with 20 to 24 caramel turtle middles, or 40 to 48, depending on the batch size you're making.

8. Remember, if you choose to just use half the batch, you can put the rest in an airtight container to store for the future. Be sure not to cover it until the caramel has completely cooled. It'll last up to 2 weeks at room temperature. To get it to liquid consistency if you are storing it for later, use 30-second, high-setting zaps in the microwave until it is liquid. Don't let it get to boiling, or it will turn very hard and chewy.

TURTLE ASSEMBLY

1. Line one or two 18×13-inch sheet pans with parchment paper, depending on the size batch of caramel you've decided on. Using a candy funnel, deposit dollops of chocolate on the parchment paper. Each one should be approximately 1½ inches in diameter, and there should be about an inch between each dollop. Make about six dollops, and then place a caramel middle on top of each one. Continue making bottoms, topping with caramel, every six or so. When you have got all your bottoms and middles done, go back to where you started and top the caramel with chocolate. You want to use enough chocolate to mostly cover the caramel. When tops are just cooled, finish by using a fork to drizzle white chocolate diagonally across the top of each turtle.

2. When turtles are completely hardened, they will last in an airtight container for 3 weeks.

DARK CHOCOLATE CRANBERRY PECAN TURTLES

This turtle brings to mind the cooler months and the holidays that follow. Get this recipe down and you're set for hostess gifts all season long!

Dark chocolate pairs beautifully with the tartness of the cranberries in this recipe. The mild sweetness of the pecans helps round this one out to make a wonderful twist on a traditional turtle. My thanks to Maria for haranguing me into making this one!

Option one ❤ premade caramel

4 cups pecans

1 ½ cups cranberries

¾ pound caramel

1 pound tempered dark chocolate

1. Line a sheet pan with parchment paper. Spread pecans in an even layer on the parchment. Sprinkle cranberries on top of pecans. Set aside.

2. Place prepared caramel into a bowl. Put bowl in microwave, and heat on high for 45 seconds to 1 minute. Take out of microwave, stir well with medium-sized spatula, and put back in for 30 seconds. At this point, your caramel should be in liquid form. A little firmer is okay!

3. Scoop a dollop of caramel from the bowl with your small silicone spatula, and using your other spatula, ease the caramel off the spatula and onto the nuts and cranberries. Try to make them anywhere from 1 ½ to 2 inches in diameter, depending on the size of the turtles you'd like to make.

4. When caramel is completely cooled, you can start assembling your turtles (see next page).

Option two ♥ homemade caramel

This batch size will make two trays of turtle middles, not one. You may always store half of the batch in an airtight container for a later project if you don't want to do a whole batch at one time.

4 cups pecans per tray

1 1/2 cups cranberries per tray

1 1/4 cups white sugar

3 tablespoons salted butter

10 ounces corn syrup (5 2-ounce scoops)

5 ounces heavy cream

1 1/2 cups evaporated milk

1/2 teaspoon salt, or more, to taste

1–2 pounds tempered dark chocolate, depending on the size batch of caramel you've decided on

1. Line two sheet pans with parchment paper. Spread pecans in an even layer on the parchment. Sprinkle cranberries on top of pecans. Set aside.

2. Place ice cream scoop in cup of cold water, and set aside.

3. Combine sugar, butter, corn syrup, and heavy cream in a heavy-bottomed saucepan, using the ice cream scoop to measure corn syrup. Over medium heat, bring to a boil, stirring gently. Place a candy thermometer into the caramel. Let it boil until it reaches 225 degrees F.

4. Add evaporated milk and stir well. At this point, the caramel will rise in the pan. Let it boil until it reduces by about half its volume. As it reduces, be sure to stir regularly, and scrape the bottom of the pan to prevent scorching. Cook until the temperature reads 230 degrees F.

5. Remove from heat.

6. Add salt. (You can add more to taste when you are assembling your turtles.) Stir gently to incorporate.

7. At this point, you can continue on as you would in the last part of option one to form the turtle middles. You'll end up with 20 to 24 caramel turtle middles, or 40 to 48, depending on the batch size you're making.

8. Remember, if you choose to just use half the batch, you can put the rest in an airtight container to store for the future. Be sure not to cover it until the caramel has completely cooled. It'll last up to two weeks at room temperature. To get it to liquid consistency if you are storing it for later, use 30-second, high-setting zaps in the microwave until it is liquid. Don't let it get to boiling, or it will turn very hard and chewy.

TURTLE ASSEMBLY

1. Line one or two 18×13-inch sheet pans with parchment paper, depending on the size batch of caramel you've decided on. Using your candy funnel, deposit dollops of chocolate on the parchment paper. Each one should be approximately 1½ inches in diameter, and there should be about an inch between each dollop. Make about six dollops, and then place a caramel middle on top of each one. Continue making bottoms, topping with caramel, every six or so. When you have got all your bottoms and middles done, go back to where you started and top the caramel with chocolate. You want to use enough chocolate to mostly cover the caramel, then finish with a swirl.

2. When turtles are completely hardened, they will last in an airtight container for 3 weeks.

CANDIED PECAN TURTLES

Another recipe that brings to mind the cooler months, this pecan turtle gets gussied up with candied nuts. Interestingly, these really taste wonderful in all three chocolate colors: white, dark, or milk. Go with your gut.

This recipe is open to shortcuts: buy the candied pecans, buy the caramel, and you can be done in no time at all. These make great gifts, but sharing is optional!

What you'll need

5 cups candied pecans (check sidebar for quick recipe, or buy your faves)

¾ pound caramel

1 pound tempered chocolate

1. Line a sheet pan with parchment paper. Spread pecans in an even layer on the parchment. Set aside.

2. Place prepared caramel into bowl. Put bowl in microwave, and heat on high for 45 seconds to 1 minute. Take out of microwave, stir well with medium-sized spatula, and put back in for 30 seconds. At this point, your caramel should be in liquid form. A little firmer is okay!

3. Scoop a dollop of caramel from the bowl with a small silicone spatula, and using your other spatula, ease the caramel off the spatula and onto the nuts. Try to make them anywhere from 1½ to 2 inches in diameter, depending on the size of the turtles you'd like to make. You'll end up with 20 to 24 turtle middles.

4. When caramel is completely cooled, you can start assembling your turtles.

TURTLE ASSEMBLY

1. Line an 18×13-inch baking sheet with parchment paper. Using your candy funnel, deposit dollops of chocolate on the parchment paper. Each one should be approximately 1½ inches in diameter, and there should be about an inch between each dollop. Make about six dollops, and then place a caramel middle on top of each one. Continue making bottoms, topping with caramel, every six or so. When you have got all your bottoms and middles done, go back to where you started and top the caramel with chocolate. You want to use enough chocolate to mostly cover the caramel, then finish with a swirl.

2. When turtles are completely hardened, they will last in an airtight container for 1 week, tops.

CANDIED PECANS

5 cups pecans
½ cup butter
½ cup brown sugar
1 teaspoon cinnamon

Line an 18×13-inch sheet pan with parchment paper.

Toast the pecans in a dry, heavy-bottomed saucepan large enough to hold all the nuts (or make this recipe in two batches, if your pan is too small), tossing to distribute heat evenly. Toast until fragrant.

Add butter, stirring to coat evenly.

When butter is melted, add brown sugar and cinnamon. Toss constantly to cover all the nuts and to prevent the sugar from burning.

Cook for about 5 to 8 minutes, and pour out onto prepared sheet pan.

Let cool completely before making your turtle middles.

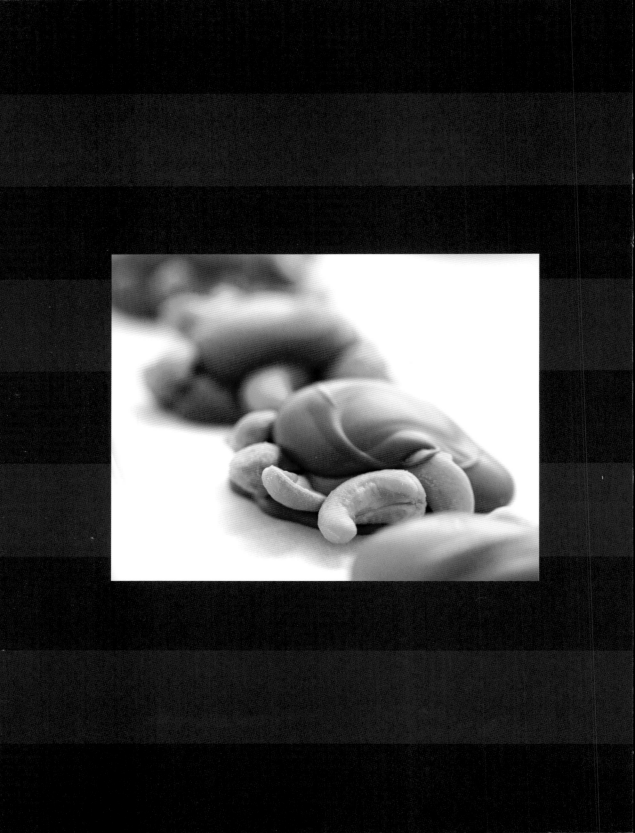

WHITE (OR DARK) CHOCOLATE CASHEW AND MANGO TURTLES

This turtle really is just as fantastic in white or dark. I don't think milk chocolate helps this recipe at all, so don't bother. I use dried mango in these turtles, but I like to spice it up when I make the dark—if you can find them, try making them with dried chili mangoes. The heat and the sweet with a buttery, salty cashew? Mon Dieu!

Option one ♥ premade caramel

5 cups roasted, salted cashews

¾ pound caramel

Dried mangoes, one slice per turtle (or chili mangoes, if you dare!)

1 pound tempered white (or dark) chocolate

1. Line a sheet pan with parchment paper. Spread cashews in an even layer on the parchment. Set aside.

2. Place prepared caramel into a bowl. Put bowl in microwave, and heat on high for 45 seconds to 1 minute. Take out of microwave, stir well with medium-sized spatula, and put back in for 30 seconds. At this point, your caramel should be in liquid form. A little firmer is okay!

3. Scoop a dollop of caramel from the bowl with a small silicone spatula, and using your other spatula, ease the caramel off the spatula and onto the nuts. Try to make them anywhere from 1½ to 2 inches in diameter, depending on the size of the turtles you'd like to make. You'll end up with 20 to 24 turtle middles.

4. When caramel is completely cooled, you can start assembling your turtles (see next page).

Option two ♥ homemade caramel

This batch size will make two trays of turtle middles, not one. You may always store half of the batch in an airtight container for a later project if you don't want to do a whole batch at one time.

5 cups cashews per tray

1¼ cups white sugar

3 tablespoons salted butter

10 ounces corn syrup (5 2-ounce scoops)

5 ounces heavy cream

1½ cups evaporated milk

Dried mangoes, one slice per turtle (or chili mangoes, if you dare!)

1–2 pounds tempered white (or dark) chocolate, depending on the size batch of caramel you've decided on

1. Line two 18×13-inch sheet pans with parchment paper. Spread cashews in an even layer on the parchment. Set aside.

2. Place ice cream scoop in cup of cold water, and set aside.

3. Combine sugar, butter, corn syrup, and heavy cream in a heavy-bottomed saucepan, using the ice cream scoop to measure corn syrup. Over medium heat, bring to a boil, stirring gently. Place candy thermometer into the caramel. Let it boil until it reaches 225 degrees F.

4. Add evaporated milk and stir well. At this point, the caramel will rise in the pan. Let it boil until it reduces by about half its volume. As it reduces, be sure to stir regularly, and scrape the bottom of the pan to prevent scorching. Cook until the temperature reads 230 degrees F.

5. Remove from heat.

6. At this point, you can continue on as you would in the last part of option one to form the turtle middles. You'll end up with 20 to 24 caramel turtle middles, or 40 to 48, depending on the batch size you're making.

7. Remember, if you choose to just use half the batch, you can put the rest in an airtight container to store for the future. Be sure not to cover it until the caramel has completely cooled. It'll last up to 2 weeks at room temperature. To get it to liquid consistency if you are storing it for later, use 30-second, high-setting zaps in the microwave until it is liquid. Don't let it get to boiling, or it will turn very hard and chewy.

TURTLE ASSEMBLY

1. Using a pair of kitchen shears, cut mangoes to about a 1½-inch length. Rinse the blades if they get too sticky. Be sure to dry thoroughly before resuming cutting. Set aside.

2. Line one or two 18×13-inch sheet pans with parchment paper. Using a candy funnel, deposit dollops of chocolate on the parchment paper. Each one should be approximately 1½ inches in diameter, and there should be about an inch between each dollop. Make about six dollops, and then place a caramel middle on top of each one. Continue making bottoms, topping with caramel, every six or so. When you have got all your bottoms and middles done, top each middle with a slice of mango. Then, go back to where you started and top the caramel with chocolate. Use enough chocolate to mostly cover the caramel, then finish with a swirl.

3. When turtles are completely hardened, they will last in an airtight container for 3 weeks.

MILK CHOCOLATE, ALMOND, AND APRICOT TURTLES

These turtles contain a flavor combination that is unexpectedly gorgeous. I really like putting these over the top with sliced, glacéed apricots. I prefer an unsalted almond for this one—I think salt tips the palate out of balance. Please do make sure the unsalted almonds are very crisp and crunchy—we want to delight our audience with a mixture of plump fruit and crunchy nuts!

Option one ♥ premade caramel

5 cups almonds

¾ pound caramel

12 glacéed apricots, sliced into thirds with kitchen shears

1 pound tempered milk chocolate

1. Line a sheet pan with parchment paper. Spread almonds in an even layer on the parchment. Set aside.

2. Place prepared caramel into bowl. Put bowl in microwave, and heat on high for 45 seconds to 1 minute. Take out of microwave, stir well with medium-sized spatula, and put back in for 30 seconds. At this point, your caramel should be in liquid form. A little firmer is okay!

3. Scoop a dollop of caramel from the bowl with a small silicone spatula, and using your other spatula, ease the caramel off the spatula and onto the nuts. Try to make them anywhere from 1½ to 2 inches in diameter, depending on the size of the turtles you'd like to make. You'll end up with 20 to 24 turtle middles.

4. When caramel is completely cooled, you can start assembling your turtles (see next page).

Option two ❤ homemade caramel

Note that this batch size will make two trays of turtle middles, not one. You may always store half of the batch in an airtight container for a later project if you don't want to do a whole batch at one time.

5 cups almonds per tray

1 1/4 cups white sugar

3 tablespoons salted butter

10 ounces corn syrup (5 2-ounce scoops)

5 ounces heavy cream

1 1/2 cups evaporated milk

1/2 teaspoon salt, or more, to taste

12–24 glacéed apricots, sliced into thirds with kitchen shears

1–2 pounds tempered milk chocolate, depending on the size batch of caramel you've decided on

1. Line one or two sheet pans with parchment paper. Spread almonds in an even layer on the parchment. Set aside.

2. Place ice cream scoop in cup of cold water, and set aside.

3. Combine sugar, butter, corn syrup, and heavy cream in a heavy-bottomed saucepan, using the ice cream scoop to measure corn syrup. Over medium heat, bring to a boil, stirring gently. Place a candy thermometer into the caramel. Let it boil until it reaches 225 degrees F.

4. Add evaporated milk and stir well. At this point, the caramel will rise in the pan. Let it boil until it reduces by about half its volume. As it reduces, be sure to stir regularly, and scrape the bottom of the pan to prevent scorching. Cook until the temperature reads 230 degrees F.

5. Remove from heat.

6. Add salt. (You can add more to taste when you are assembling your turtles.) Stir gently to incorporate.

7. At this point, you can continue on as you would in the last part of option one to form the turtle middles. You'll end up with 20 to 24 caramel turtle middles, or 40 to 48, depending on the batch size you're making.

8. Remember, if you choose to just use half the batch, you can put the rest in an airtight container to store for the future. Be sure not to cover it until the caramel has completely cooled. It'll last up to two weeks at room temperature. To get it to liquid consistency if you are storing it for later, use 30-second, high-setting zaps in the microwave until it is liquid. Don't let it get to boiling, or it will turn very hard and chewy.

TURTLE ASSEMBLY

1. Line one or two 18×13-inch sheet pans with parchment paper. Using a candy funnel, deposit dollops of chocolate on the parchment paper. Each one should be approximately 1 ½ inches in diameter, and there should be about an inch between each dollop. Make about six dollops, and then place a caramel middle on top of each one. Continue making bottoms, topping with caramel, every six or so. When you have got all your bottoms and middles done, top each middle with two slices of apricot. Then, go back to where you started and top the caramel with chocolate. You want to use enough chocolate to mostly cover the caramel, then finish with a swirl.

2. When turtles are completely hardened, they will last in an airtight container for 3 weeks.

WHITE CHOCOLATE BLUEBERRY ORANGE PECAN TURTLES

These babies just say summer—bright dried blueberries, sweet pecans, and white chocolate, topped with a sliver of candied orange peel. Sweet and sophisticated, these are perfect with a well-chilled glass of Prosecco.

Make sure your pecans are raw and unsalted; this makes an enormous difference when layering these particular flavors.

Option one ♥ premade caramel

> 4 ½ cups raw pecans
>
> 1 ½ cups dried blueberries
>
> ¾ pound caramel
>
> Candied orange peel (enough to top each turtle)
>
> 1 pound tempered white chocolate

1. Line a sheet pan with parchment paper. Spread pecans in an even layer on the parchment. Sprinkle blueberries on top of pecans. Set aside.

2. Place prepared caramel into bowl. Put bowl in microwave, and heat on high for 45 seconds to 1 minute. Take out of microwave, stir well with medium-sized spatula, and put back in for 30 seconds. At this point, your caramel should be in liquid form. A little firmer is okay!

3. Scoop a dollop of caramel from the bowl with a small silicone spatula, and using your other spatula, ease the caramel off the spatula and onto the nuts and berries. Try to make them anywhere from 1 ½ to 2 inches in diameter, depending on the size of the turtles you'd like to make. You'll end up with 20 to 24 turtle middles.

4. When caramel is completely cooled, you can start assembling your turtles (see next page).

Option two ❤ homemade caramel

Note that this batch size will make two trays of turtle middles, not one. You may always store half of the batch in an airtight container for a later project if you don't want to do a whole batch at one time.

> 4 ½ cups pecans per tray
>
> 1 ½ cups blueberries per tray
>
> 1 ¼ cups white sugar
>
> 3 tablespoons salted butter
>
> 10 ounces corn syrup (5 2-ounce scoops)
>
> 5 ounces heavy cream
>
> 1 ½ cups evaporated milk
>
> ½ teaspoon salt, or more, to taste
>
> Candied orange peel (enough to top each turtle)
>
> 1–2 pounds tempered white chocolate, depending on the size batch of caramel you've decided on

1. Line one or two 18×13-inch sheet pans with parchment paper. Spread pecans in an even layer on the parchment. Sprinkle blueberries on top of pecans. Set aside.

2. Place ice cream scoop in cup of cold water, and set aside.

3. Combine sugar, butter, corn syrup, and heavy cream in a heavy-bottomed saucepan, using the ice cream scoop to measure corn syrup. Over medium heat, bring to a boil, stirring gently. Place a candy thermometer into the caramel. Let it boil until it reaches 225 degrees F.

4. Add evaporated milk and stir well. At this point, the caramel will rise in the pan. Let it boil until it reduces by about half its volume. As it reduces, be sure to stir regularly, and scrape the bottom of the pan to prevent scorching. Cook until the temperature reads 230 degrees F.

5. Remove from heat.

6. Add salt. (You can add more to taste when you are assembling your turtles.) Stir gently to incorporate.

7. At this point, you can continue on as you would in the last part option one to form the turtle middles. You'll end up with 20 to 24 caramel turtle middles, or 40 to 48, depending on the batch size you're making.

8. Remember, if you choose to just use half the batch, you can put the rest in an airtight container to store for the future. Be sure not to cover it until the caramel has completely cooled. It'll last up to 2 weeks at room temperature. To get it to liquid consistency if you are storing it for later, use 30-second, high-setting zaps in the microwave until it is liquid. Don't let it get to boiling, or it will turn very hard and chewy.

TURTLE ASSEMBLY

1. Using kitchen shears, cut the orange peel to 1-inch lengths. Rinse the blades if they get too sticky. Be sure to dry thoroughly before resuming cutting. Set aside.

2. Line one or two 18×13-inch sheet pans with parchment paper. Using your candy funnel, deposit dollops of chocolate on the parchment paper. Each one should be approximately 1 ½ inches in diameter, and there should be about an inch between each dollop. Make about six dollops, and then place a caramel middle on top of each one. Continue making bottoms, topping with caramel, every six or so. When you have got all your bottoms and middles done, go back to where you started and top the caramel with chocolate. Top with each turtle with one slice of orange peel.

3. When turtles are completely hardened, they will last in an airtight container for 3 weeks.

FRUIT CUP TURTLES

Eek! A turtle without nuts? Well, why the hell not?

These days, we've got such an assortment of dried fruits to choose from, it boggles the mind. I can't get enough of those dried tart cherries, so let's throw those in, along with chopped papaya and a bit of chopped, candied lemon peel. Let's pretend these turtles are health food, and top them with toasted pumpkin seeds.

Chocolate color? Choose your poison. There is absolutely no way to do these wrong.

Take two of these and call me in the morning!

Option one ♥ premade caramel

2 cups dried tart cherries

2 cups chopped papaya

1 cup chopped lemon peel

¾ pound caramel

1 pound tempered chocolate

½ cup roasted, salted pumpkin seeds

1. Line a sheet pan with parchment paper. Spread cherries in an even layer on the parchment. Layer papaya on top of the cherries. Sprinkle lemon peel on top of cherries and papaya. Set aside.

2. Place prepared caramel into a bowl. Put bowl in microwave, and heat on high for 45 seconds to 1 minute. Take out of microwave, stir well with medium-sized spatula, and put back in for 30 seconds. At this point, your caramel should be in liquid form.

3. Scoop a dollop of caramel from the bowl with your small silicone spatula, and using your other spatula, ease the caramel off the spatula and onto the fruit. Try to make them anywhere from 1½ to 2 inches in diameter, depending on the size of the turtles you'd like to make. You'll end up with 20 to 24 caramel turtle middles.

4. When caramel is completely cooled, you can start assembling your turtles.

Option two ❤ homemade caramel

This batch size will make two trays of turtle middles, not one. You may always store half of the batch in an airtight container for a later project if you don't want to do a whole batch at one time.

2 cups dried tart cherries

2 cups chopped papaya

1 cup chopped lemon peel

1 ¼ cups white sugar

3 tablespoons salted butter

10 ounces corn syrup (5 2-ounce scoops)

5 ounces heavy cream

1 ½ cups evaporated milk

½ teaspoon salt, or more, to taste

1–2 pounds tempered chocolate, depending on the size batch of caramel you've decided on

½ cup roasted, salted pumpkin seeds

1. Line one or two 18×13-inch sheet pans with parchment paper. Spread cherries in an even layer on the parchment. Layer papaya on top of the cherries. Sprinkle lemon on top of the papaya and cherries. Set aside.

2. Place ice cream scoop in cup of cold water, and set aside.

3. Combine sugar, butter, corn syrup, and heavy cream in a heavy-bottomed saucepan, using the ice cream scoop to measure corn syrup. Over medium heat, bring to a boil, stirring gently. Place a candy thermometer into the caramel. Let it boil until it reaches 225 degrees F.

4. Add evaporated milk and stir well. At this point, the caramel will rise in the pan. Let it boil until it reduces by about half its volume. As it reduces, be sure to stir regularly, and scrape the bottom of the pan to prevent scorching. Cook until the temperature reads 230 degrees F.

5. Remove from heat.

6. Add salt. (You can add more to taste when you are assembling your turtles.) Stir gently to incorporate.

7. At this point, you can continue on as you would in the last part of option one to form the turtle middles. You'll end up with 20 to 24 caramel turtle middles, or 40 to 48, depending on the batch size you're making.

8. Remember, if you choose to just use half the batch, you can put the rest in an airtight container to store for the future. Be sure not to cover it until the caramel has completely cooled. It'll last up to 2 weeks at room temperature. To get it to liquid consistency if you are storing it for later, use 30-second, high-setting zaps in the micro-wave until it is liquid. Don't let it get to boiling, or it will turn very hard and chewy.

TURTLE ASSEMBLY

1. Line one or two 18×13-inch sheet pans with parchment paper. Using a candy funnel, deposit dollops of chocolate on the parchment paper. Each one should be approximately 1½ inches in diameter, and there should be about an inch between each dollop. Make about six dollops, and then place a caramel middle on top of each one. Continue making bottoms, topping with caramel, every six or so. When you have got all your bottoms and middles done, go back to where you started and top the caramel with chocolate. You want to use enough chocolate to mostly cover the caramel. Sprinkle pumpkin seeds on top.

2. When turtles are completely hardened, they will last in an airtight container for 3 weeks.

MILK CHOCOLATE PEANUT TURTLES

It's really simple. Peanuts and milk chocolate are perfect for each other. This turtle I like to keep completely fuss-free. Great big roasted, salted peanuts with rich, sweet milk chocolate. This turtle really deserves our handmade caramel. No two ways about it, people.

This caramel batch size will make two trays of turtle middles, not one. You can always store half of the batch in an airtight container for a later project if you don't want to do a whole batch at one time.

What you'll need

5 cups roasted, salted peanuts per tray

1¼ cups white sugar

3 tablespoons salted butter

10 ounces corn syrup (5 2-ounce scoops)

5 ounces heavy cream

1½ cups evaporated milk

½ teaspoon salt, or more to taste

1–2 pounds tempered milk chocolate, depending on batch size

1. Line one or two 18×13-inch sheet pans with parchment paper. Spread peanuts in an even layer on the parchment. Set aside.

2. Place ice cream scoop in cup of cold water, and set aside.

3. Combine sugar, butter, corn syrup, and heavy cream in a heavy-bottomed saucepan, using the ice cream scoop to measure the corn syrup. Over medium heat, bring to a boil, stirring gently. Place a candy thermometer into the caramel. Let it boil until it reaches 225 degrees F.

4. Add evaporated milk and stir well. At this point, the caramel will rise in the pan. Let it boil until it reduces by about half its volume. As it reduces, be sure to stir regularly, and scrape the bottom of the pan to prevent scorching. Cook until the temperature reads 230 degrees F.

5. Remove from heat.

6. Add salt. (You can add more to taste when you are assembling your turtles.) Stir gently to incorporate.

7. Remember, if you choose to just use half the batch, you can put the rest in an airtight container to store for the future. Be sure not to cover it until the caramel has completely cooled. It'll last up to 2 weeks at room temperature.

8. Scoop a dollop of caramel from the bowl with a small silicone spatula, and using your other spatula, ease the caramel off the spatula and onto the nuts. Try to make the caramel about 1 ½ to 2 inches in diameter, depending on the size of the turtles you'd like to make. You'll end up with 20 to 24 caramel turtle middles, or 40 to 48, depending on batch size.

TURTLE ASSEMBLY

1. Line one or two 18×13-inch sheet pans with parchment paper. Using a candy funnel, deposit dollops of chocolate on the parchment paper. Each one should be approximately 1 ½ inches in diameter, and there should be about an inch between each dollop. Make about six dollops, and then place a caramel middle on top of each one. Continue making bottoms, topping with caramel, every six or so. When you have got all your bottoms and middles done, go back to where you started and top the caramel with chocolate. You want to use enough chocolate to mostly cover the caramel, and finish with a swirl.

2. When turtles are completely hardened, they will last in an airtight container for 2 weeks.

MILK CHOCOLATE BRAZIL NUT TURTLES

These get put together a little differently from the turtles we've been making. Brazil nuts are so large, just one seems perfect to round out the turtle trinity of ingredients. Brazil nuts have a really subtle flavor, so we are making these in milk chocolate. The simplicity of a Brazil nut really calls for homemade caramel, in my opinion. If you'd like, chop extra nuts to sprinkle on top.

What you'll need

1¼ cups white sugar

3 tablespoons salted butter

10 ounces corn syrup (5 2-ounce scoops)

5 ounces heavy cream

1½ cups evaporated milk

20–24 Brazil nuts, or 40–48, depending on the caramel batch size

1–2 pounds tempered milk chocolate, depending on batch size

Extra chopped Brazil nuts for garnish, if desired

1. Line one or two 18×13-inch sheet pans with parchment paper. Set aside.

2. Place ice cream scoop in cup of cold water, and set aside.

3. Combine sugar, butter, corn syrup, and heavy cream in a heavy-bottomed saucepan, using the ice cream scoop to measure corn syrup. Over medium heat, bring to a boil, stirring gently. Place a candy thermometer into the caramel. Let it boil until it reaches 225 degrees F.

4. Add evaporated milk and stir well. At this point, the caramel will rise in the pan. Let it boil until it reduces by about half its volume. As it reduces, be sure to stir regularly, and scrape the bottom of the pan to prevent scorching. Cook until the temperature reads 230 degrees F.

5. Remove from heat. (Remember, if you choose to just use half the batch, you can put the rest in an airtight container to store for the future. Be sure not to cover it until the caramel has completely cooled. It'll last up to 2 weeks at room temperature.)

6. Scoop a dollop of caramel from the bowl with your small silicone spatula, and using your other spatula, ease the caramel off the spatula onto the parchment paper. Try to make the caramel about 1 inch in diameter. You'll end up with 20 to 24 (or 40 to 48, depending on batch size) caramel turtle middles.

7. While the caramel is still warm, lightly set a Brazil nut in the center of each caramel dollop. Let it cool completely.

8. When ready to assemble turtles, loosen Brazil nut/caramel middles from parchment paper. (I find it's easiest to flip the parchment over onto another piece of parchment. Let it sit for 10 minutes, and snap the caramel middles off the paper.)

TURTLE ASSEMBLY

1. Line one or two 18×13-inch sheet pans with parchment paper. Using a candy funnel, deposit dollops of chocolate on the parchment paper. Each one should be approximately 1½ inches in diameter, and there should be about an inch between each dollop. Make about six dollops, and then place a caramel middle on top of each one. Continue making bottoms, topping with caramel, every six or so. When you have got all your bottoms and middles done, go back to where you started and top the caramel with chocolate. You want to use enough chocolate to mostly cover the caramel, and finish with a swirl, or top with a sprinkle of chopped Brazil nuts.

2. When turtles are completely hardened, they will last in an airtight container for 2 weeks.

Truffles have always conveyed luxury to me—whether it's the inclusion of posh ingredients, or just the simple richness of texture and taste, I can never tell. This last section combines Master Recipe Three for truffles with our first Master Recipe. Take your time. Read the recipes through, and then get busy!

truffles

TRUFFLES

Our base recipe for a truffle is as simple as it is elegant: only three ingredients! Be sure your three are the best you can find—your choices will make these truffles truly yours.

Truffles are a two-day project; the first day the truffles get made, and the second day they get rolled, or cut, and dipped. On day two, there are two options to finish the truffles: the first one is the traditional way, rolling the truffle in a cocoa/sugar mixture. Option two is a bit more complicated, as it involves dipping the truffle in chocolate.

Specialized kitchen utensils and equipment you'll need

DAY ONE

Heavy-bottomed saucepan

2 silicone spatulas, one small, one medium

Whisk

9×9-inch baking pan, lined with parchment paper (make sure parchment paper hangs over all four edges of pan, so you can lift the truffles out)

One more sheet of parchment paper

DAY TWO, OPTION ONE (ROLLED TRUFFLES)

Shallow bowl

Small melon baller

18×13-inch baking sheet lined with parchment paper

Candy cups

DAY TWO, OPTION TWO (CUT TRUFFLES)

Offset spatula

Parchment paper

Chef's knife

Butter knife

Dipping fork, or regular fork

2 18×13-inch sheet pans, both lined with parchment paper

Candy cups

What you'll need

2 ounces butter

¾ cup light cream

1 ½ pounds tempered chocolate

1. Over low heat, melt butter into cream in a heavy-bottomed sauce-pan. Use a small silicone spatula to stir gently all the while. When the butter has completely been incorporated into the cream, remove from heat.

2. Slowly pour a medium-sized stream of tempered chocolate into the cream and butter mixture, whisking constantly. Scrape every last bit of chocolate out and into your cream mixture! More chocolate equals more richness.

3. Using a medium spatula, pour the truffle mixture into a parchment-lined, 9×9-inch baking pan.

4. Let cool completely, drape a piece of parchment paper over the top of the pan (do not wrap tightly—truffles need to breathe), and leave out at room temperature (not warmer than 70 degrees F) overnight.

DAY TWO

Option one ♥ rolled truffles

2 tablespoons unsweetened cocoa, plus more for dusting hands, melon baller, and truffles

1 tablespoon granulated white sugar (powdered sugar works great too; it's all about what you want from the texture of the truffle—I love the little bit of crunch granulated sugar adds, but if you're a purist and just want smooth and silky, go with powdered)

1. Put 2 tablespoons unsweetened cocoa in a shallow bowl. Add 1 table-spoon sugar. Set aside.

2. Dust the top of the truffles with additional cocoa.

continued …

3. Coat a melon baller in cocoa, then scoop truffle mixture into a ball. Drop ball into shallow bowl of cocoa and sugar, and roll around until completely covered. Place truffle on a parchment-lined baking sheet. Repeat until truffle mixture is used up.

4. When the truffles have rested for a bit, they can be put into candy cups and served, or stored in an airtight container for up to one week.

Option two ❤ cut truffles

½ pound tempered chocolate

Unsweetened cocoa for dusting hands, knife, and truffles

3–5 pounds tempered chocolate in a bowl, for dipping
(I recommend you temper chocolate 1 pound at a time, to keep it from going out of temper)

1. Using an offset spatula, spread ½ pound tempered chocolate over truffles in the 9×9-inch baking pan. Spread it as thinly and as uniformly as you can. Spread the parchment paper over the wet chocolate. This will end up being the bottom of the truffle.

2. When chocolate is completely cooled and hard, lift truffles out of pan. Place the bottom of the pan on top of the cooled chocolate side (the bottom), and flip over carefully. Slide the truffles off the bottom of the pan onto your countertop. Carefully peel the parchment paper off the top of the truffle.

3. Lightly dust truffles with cocoa, then dust your hands and both sides of a chef's knife.

4. Score truffles with chef's knife, looking to make 1×1-inch squares.

5. Cover both sides of the chef's knife with cocoa, and cut a strip of truffles. Scrape the sides of the chef's knife with a butter knife, coat with cocoa, and cut another strip of truffles.

6. Cut into squares, and place (with cocoa-covered fingers so they don't stick to you!) on parchment-lined baking sheet. Continue cutting until all the truffles have been portioned out. Wipe the butter knife clean when finished; you'll need it again.

7. Place a truffle on a dipping fork (or regular fork). Tap lightly to dislodge any extra cocoa, then dip into the tempered chocolate. When your truffle has been dipped, tap the dipping fork gently on the side of the bowl to let any extra chocolate drip off. Using the butter knife to help with the transfer, tip the truffle onto the sheet pan. If you find your truffle is swimming in a sea of chocolate after you put it down, there's a bit too much chocolate. Next time, tap the excess chocolate off more thoroughly. That first one is for you to eat!

8. Let cool until completely dry, and place in candy cups. These will last up to 3 weeks in an airtight container.

CAN'T TOUCH THIS!

Truffles have the potential to be truly hellish when handling. There are a few things you can do to make it less of a trial:

First, keep your tools clean. That means scrape down any tools as you work, the minute they get mucked up. Truffle buildup on a knife spells disaster if you're looking for a crisp, clean square truffle to dip. I can't tell you how many times I've thought, "I'll just get one more cut out of this before I clean it," only to be cursing minutes later.

Second, and maybe most importantly, time is on your side. Patience really is a virtue when dealing with truffles. After you've flipped over your chocolate-bottomed truffles, but before you cut—walk away. Get a cup of tea, pour a glass of wine, whatever. Truffles are so much easier to handle after they've been exposed to air. This is true when you're scooping truffles to roll, too. If your truffle mixture is too loose, let it get some air!

Last, do you remember the saying "cool hands, warm heart"? Keep your hands cool when handling, and your tools should be cool too (don't rinse with hot water!). Truffles are the petite flower of chocolates—very sensitive. Your hot hands or knife can really complicate an otherwise straightforward process.

DARK CHOCOLATE NUT TRUFFLES

This rolled truffle leaves room for expression; the choice of nut is up to you! I will say, when choosing, it's best to pick a nut that is only very lightly salted— we're going to roll the truffle in the nuts. A little salt is fine, but too much will take away from the deep simplicity of a dark truffle. Also, if you choose a nut that hasn't been roasted, it does the nuts a bit of good to toast them gently on the stovetop in a dry frying pan until fragrant.

I love a pistachio for this, or a hazelnut. Traditionally, you'll see these done in crushed walnuts, which is lovely as well.

What you'll need

2 ounces butter

¾ cup light cream

1 ½ pounds tempered dark chocolate

1. Over low heat, melt butter into cream in a heavy-bottomed saucepan. Use a small silicone spatula to stir gently. When the butter has completely melted into the cream, remove from heat.

2. Slowly pour a medium-sized stream of tempered chocolate into the cream and butter mixture, whisking constantly.

3. Using a medium spatula, pour the truffle mixture into a parchment-lined, 9×9-inch baking pan.

4. Let cool completely, drape a piece of parchment paper over the top of the pan (do not wrap tightly—truffles need to breathe), and leave out at room temperature (not warmer than 70 degrees F) overnight.

DAY TWO

What you'll need

¾ cup chopped nut of your choice

Unsweetened cocoa for dusting hands and melon baller

1. Put chopped nuts in a shallow bowl. Set aside.

2. There's no need to dust the top of these truffles with cocoa. We want them a bit sticky so the nuts stay on.

3. Coat a melon baller in cocoa, then scoop truffle mixture into a ball. Drop ball into shallow bowl of nuts, and roll around until completely covered (you may have to pat the nuts into the truffle to adhere them). Place truffle on a parchment-lined baking sheet. Repeat until truffle mixture is used up.

4. When the truffles have rested for a bit, they can be put into candy cups and served, or stored in an airtight container for up to 1 week.

RUM TRUFFLES (MILK OR DARK)

These are a favorite at the holidays, but I like them all winter long. Lovely served with espresso or oolong tea. Choose the deepest, darkest rum you can find. If you're unsure, you may have to unleash your inner pirate and do some serious taste testing. Aarrrrr!

I like these just simply rolled in cocoa and a bit of powdered sugar. We don't want anything to take away from the rum, do we?

What you'll need

2 ounces butter

¾ cup light cream

1 ½ pounds tempered milk or dark chocolate

2 ½ tablespoons dark rum

1. Over low heat, melt butter into cream in a heavy-bottomed saucepan. Use a small silicone spatula to stir gently all the while. When the butter has completely been incorporated into the cream, remove from heat.

2. Slowly pour a medium-sized stream of tempered chocolate into the cream and butter mixture, whisking constantly. When chocolate is completely mixed in, whisk in rum.

3. Using a medium spatula, pour the truffle mixture into a parchment-lined, 9×9-inch baking pan.

4. Let cool completely, drape a piece of parchment paper over the top of the pan, and leave out at room temperature (not warmer than 70 degrees F) overnight.

DAY TWO

What you'll need

2 tablespoons unsweetened cocoa, plus extra for dusting hands and melon baller

½ tablespoon powdered sugar

1. Combine cocoa and sugar in a shallow bowl. Set aside.

2. Coat a melon baller in additional cocoa, then scoop truffle mixture into a ball. Drop ball into shallow bowl of cocoa and sugar, and roll around until completely covered. Place truffle on a parchment-lined baking sheet. Repeat until truffle mixture is used up.

3. When the truffles have rested for a bit, they can be put into candy cups and served, or stored in an airtight container for up to 1 week.

Turtle, Truffle, Bark!

DARK CHOCOLATE MINT TRUFFLES

This classic combination deserves your deepest, darkest chocolate—no excuses! I really like this one dipped in dark, as well, with lots of bracing peppermint flavor. For the holiday season, however, it's fun and festive to roll them in crushed candy canes for a really over-the-top minty explosion with tons of texture. If that's too much, you can always sprinkle a little crushed candy cane on top of each dipped truffle as you go. You decide. Both options will be covered in this recipe.

DAY ONE

What you'll need

> **2 ounces butter**
>
> **¾ cup light cream**
>
> **1 ½ pounds tempered dark chocolate**
>
> **½ teaspoon peppermint oil**

1. Over low heat, melt butter into cream. Use your small silicone spatula to stir gently all the while. When the butter has completely been incorporated into the cream, remove from heat.

2. Slowly pour a medium-sized stream of tempered chocolate into the cream and butter mixture, whisking constantly. When chocolate is completely mixed in, whisk in peppermint oil.

3. Using the medium spatula, pour the truffle mixture into the parchment-lined, 9×9-inch baking pan.

4. Let cool completely, loosely drape a piece of parchment paper over the top of the pan, and leave out at room temperature (not warmer than 70 degrees F) overnight.

Option one ♥ rolled truffles

¾ cup crushed candy canes

Unsweetened cocoa for dusting hands and melon baller

1. Put candy canes in a shallow bowl. Set aside.

2. Coat a melon baller in cocoa, then scoop truffle mixture into a ball. Drop ball into shallow bowl of crushed candy canes, and roll around until completely covered. Place truffle on a parchment-lined baking sheet. Repeat until truffle mixture is used up.

3. When the truffles have rested for a bit, they can be put into candy cups and served, or stored in an airtight container for up to 1 week.

Option two ♥ cut truffles

½ pound tempered dark chocolate

Unsweetened cocoa for dusting hands, knife, truffles

3–5 pounds tempered dark chocolate in a bowl, for dipping (I recommend you temper chocolate 1 pound at a time, to keep it from going out of temper)

½ cup crushed candy canes

1. Using an offset spatula, spread ½ pound tempered chocolate over truffles in the 9×9-inch pan. Spread it as thinly and as uniformly as you can. Spread parchment paper over the wet chocolate. This will end up being the bottom of the truffle.

2. When chocolate is completely cooled and hard, lift truffles out of pan. Place the bottom of the pan on top of the cooled chocolate side (the bottom), and flip over carefully. Slide the truffles off the bottom of the pan onto your countertop. Carefully peel the parchment paper off the top of the truffle.

3. Lightly dust truffles with cocoa, then dust your hands, and both sides of a chef's knife.

4. Score truffles with knife, looking to make 1×1-inch squares.

5. Cover both sides of the knife with cocoa and cut a strip of truffles. Scrape the sides of the chef's knife with a butter knife, coat with cocoa, and cut another strip of truffles.

6. Cut into squares, and place on a parchment-lined baking sheet. Continue cutting until all the truffles have been portioned out. Wipe the butter knife clean when finished; you'll need it again.

7. Place a truffle on a dipping fork. Tap lightly to dislodge any extra cocoa, then dip into the tempered chocolate. After dipping, tap the fork gently on the side of the bowl to let any excess chocolate drip off. Using the butter knife to help with the transfer, tip the truffle onto the sheet pan.

8. Before they dry, lightly sprinkle crushed candy canes on top. If the truffles get too dry before they get sprinkled, the candy canes may not stick, so be sure to sprinkle as you go!

9. When totally dry, place in candy cups and store in an airtight container for up to 3 weeks.

10. For the holidays, it's fun to dress these up with special patterned candy cups. These are presented beautifully in a decorative tin, which also helps keep all that delightful peppermint flavor inside!

MILK CHOCOLATE, NUTMEG, AND CLOVE TRUFFLES

While I generally like spiced truffles dipped in chocolate, these are really elegant rolled in slivered almonds. Choose super fresh, unsalted almonds—you can buy them pre-slivered, or chop your own. If you buy pre-slivered ones, do taste before using. Sometimes they can be a bit lackluster in the flavor department. Your taste buds will let you know which to use!

DAY ONE

What you'll need

2 ounces butter

¾ cup light cream

1½ pounds tempered milk chocolate

½ teaspoon nutmeg

¼ teaspoon cloves

1. Over low heat, melt butter into cream. Use a small silicone spatula to stir gently. When the butter has completely melted into the cream, remove from heat.

2. Slowly pour a medium-sized stream of tempered chocolate into the cream and butter mixture, whisking constantly. When chocolate is fully incorporated, whisk in spices.

3. Using a medium spatula, pour the truffle mixture into a parchment-lined, 9×9-inch baking pan.

4. Let cool completely, drape a piece of parchment paper over the top of the pan, and leave out at room temperature (not warmer than 70 degrees F) overnight.

What you'll need

½ – ¾ cup slivered or chopped almonds

1 teaspoon orange zest, optional

Unsweetened cocoa for dusting hands and melon baller

1. Put almonds in a shallow bowl. Add orange zest if desired. Set aside.

2. Coat a melon baller in cocoa, then scoop truffle mixture into a ball. Drop ball into shallow bowl of nuts, and roll around until completely covered. The shape of the almonds may make it necessary for you to pat the almonds into the truffle mixture. Do so gently, and wipe your hands clean often, so the chocolate on your fingers doesn't mar the look of the almonds. Place truffle on parchment-lined baking sheet. Repeat until truffle mixture is used up.

3. When the truffles have rested for a bit, they can be put into candy cups and served, or stored in an airtight container for up to 1 week.

MOCHA TRUFFLES

I don't think I've ever met anyone who isn't entranced with mocha. It's classic because it's just too hard to resist! In this recipe, we use coffee extract to mix into milk chocolate. There are really nice extracts out there nowadays, and the strength of the extract is mellowed by the milk chocolate. I like this one dipped in dark, but you are more than welcome to dip in milk.

DAY ONE

What you'll need

2 ounces butter

¾ cup light cream

1½ pounds tempered milk chocolate

½ teaspoon coffee extract (¾ teaspoon, if you really want a whack of flavor)

1. Over low heat, melt butter into cream in a heavy-bottomed saucepan. Use a small silicone spatula to stir gently all the while. When the butter has completely been incorporated into the cream, remove from heat.

2. Slowly pour a medium-sized stream of tempered chocolate into the cream and butter mixture, whisking constantly. When chocolate is completely mixed in, whisk in extract.

3. Using a medium spatula, pour the truffle mixture into a parchment-lined, 9×9-inch baking pan.

4. Let cool completely, drape a piece of parchment paper over the top of the pan, and leave out at room temperature (not warmer than 70 degrees F) overnight.

What you'll need

½ pound tempered milk chocolate

Unsweetened cocoa for dusting hands, knife, and truffles

3–5 pounds tempered dark chocolate in a bowl, for dipping
(I recommend you temper chocolate 1 pound at a time, to keep
it from going out of temper)

1. Using an offset spatula, spread ½ pound tempered chocolate over truffles in the 9×9-inch baking pan. Spread it as thinly and as uniformly as you can. Spread the parchment paper over the wet chocolate. This will end up being the bottom of the truffle.

2. When chocolate is completely cooled and hard, lift truffles out of pan. Place the bottom of the pan on top of the cooled chocolate side (the bottom), and flip over carefully. Slide the truffles off the bottom of the pan onto your countertop. Carefully peel the parchment paper off the top of the truffle.

3. Lightly dust truffles with cocoa, then dust your hands and both sides of a chef's knife.

4. Score truffles with knife, looking to make 9×9-inch squares.

5. Cover both sides of the knife with cocoa, and cut a strip of truffles. Scrape the sides of the chef's knife with a butter knife, coat with cocoa, and cut another strip of truffles.

6. Cut into squares and place on a parchment-lined baking sheet. Continue cutting until all the truffles have been portioned out. Wipe the butter knife clean when finished; you'll need it again.

7. Place a truffle on your dipping fork. Tap lightly to dislodge any extra cocoa, then dip into the tempered chocolate. After dipping, tap the fork gently on the side of the bowl to let any excess chocolate drip off. Using the butter knife to help with the transfer, tip the truffle onto the sheet pan.

8. While the truffles are still wet, sprinkle with chocolate sprinkles, if desired. When they are fully dry, place in candy cups. These can be stored in an airtight container for up to 3 weeks.

LICENSE TO PLAY!

These rolled truffles offer a lot in the creative arena: if you find really great colored sprinkles, roll in them! Just recently I found tiny star sprinkles and put them on just about everything I could get my hands on. If you've got a color scheme going on, alter your recipe to roll in sprinkles that match. No holds barred!

Also, recipes with rolled nuts can get the elegance pumped up even more by adding a tiny bit of fruit zest to the nut mixture. In this recipe, I would happily zest a quarter of an orange (about a teaspoon of zest) to add to this. The play of a little citrus brightness in a richly spiced truffle is, well, stupendous.

MILK CHOCOLATE COCONUT CURRY TRUFFLES

Put curry in anything and you'll have my heart. Despite how busy this truffle sounds, we go easy on the curry to develop a more subtle flavor, then roll in shredded coconut. I love to make this with a hot curry, but that's not for everyone, so I really recommend using Maharajah curry. It's sweet, but still packs a true curry punch, flavor-wise. The coconut should be unsweetened, so it doesn't compete too much with the curry. What we're looking for here is balance.

DAY ONE

What you'll need

2 ounces butter

¾ cup light cream

1½ pounds tempered milk chocolate

1 teaspoon Maharajah curry

1. Over low heat, melt butter into cream in a heavy-bottomed saucepan. Use a small silicone spatula to stir gently. When the butter has completely melted into the cream, remove from heat.

2. Slowly pour a medium-sized stream of tempered chocolate into the cream and butter mixture, whisking constantly. When chocolate is fully incorporated, whisk in curry. Using a medium spatula, pour the truffle mixture into a parchment-lined, 9×9-inch baking pan.

3. Let cool completely, drape a piece of parchment paper over the top of the pan (do not wrap tightly—truffles need to breathe), and leave out at room temperature (not warmer than 70 degrees F) overnight.

What you'll need

¾ cup unsweetened coconut, shredded

Unsweetened cocoa for dusting hands and melon baller

1. Put coconut in a shallow bowl. Set aside.

2. Coat a melon baller in cocoa, then scoop truffle mixture into a ball. Drop ball into coconut, and roll around until completely covered. Place truffle on parchment-lined baking sheet. Repeat until truffle mixture is used up.

3. When the truffles have rested for a bit, they can be put into candy cups and served, or stored in an airtight container for up to 1 week.

RASPBERRY TRUFFLES

This is by far one of my favorite truffles. I can't resist a raspberry, ever, and pairing it with dark chocolate only makes it more delightful. Sweet, tart, deep, dark—nothing wrong there!

Take the time to find a really nice puree. We'll dip these in a crisp shell of deep, dark chocolate. Heaven!

DAY ONE

What you'll need

2 ounces butter

¾ cup light cream

1 ½ pounds tempered dark chocolate

2 ½ tablespoons raspberry mash or puree (be sure to push through a sieve to remove seeds, if there are any)

1. Over low heat, melt butter into cream in a heavy-bottomed sauce-pan. Use a small silicone spatula to stir gently all the while. When the butter has completely been incorporated into the cream, remove from heat.

2. Slowly pour a medium-sized stream of tempered chocolate into the cream and butter mixture, whisking constantly. Make sure there are no lumps in your raspberry puree, then whisk it into the truffle mix.

3. Using a medium spatula, pour the truffle mixture into the parchment-lined, 9×9-inch baking pan.

4. Let cool completely, drape a piece of parchment paper over the top of the pan, and leave out at room temperature (not warmer than 70 degrees F) overnight.

What you'll need

½ pound tempered dark chocolate

Unsweetened cocoa for dusting hands, knife, and truffles

3–5 pounds tempered dark chocolate in a bowl, for dipping
(I recommend you temper chocolate 1 pound at a time, to keep
it from going out of temper)

Fresh raspberries for garnish, optional

1. Using an offset spatula, spread ½ pound tempered chocolate over truffles in the 9×9-inch pan. Spread it as thinly and as uniformly as you can. Spread parchment paper over the wet chocolate. This will end up being the bottom of the truffle.

2. When chocolate is completely cooled and hard, lift truffles out of pan. Place the bottom of the pan on top of the cooled chocolate side (the bottom), and flip over carefully. Slide the truffles off the bottom of the pan onto your countertop. Carefully peel the parchment paper off the top of the truffle.

3. Lightly dust truffles with cocoa, then dust your hands and both sides of a chef's knife.

4. Score truffles with knife, looking to make 1×1-inch squares.

5. Cover both sides of the knife with cocoa, and cut a strip of truffles. Scrape the sides of the chef's knife with a butter knife, coat with cocoa, and cut another strip of truffles.

6. Cut into squares and place (with cocoa-covered fingers so they don't stick to you!) on a parchment-lined baking sheet. Continue cutting until all the truffles have been portioned out. Wipe the butter knife clean when finished; you'll need it again.

continued . . .

7. Place a truffle on a dipping fork. Tap lightly to dislodge any extra cocoa, then dip into the chocolate. After dipping, tap the fork gently on the side of the bowl to let any excess chocolate drip off. Using the butter knife to help with the transfer, tip the truffle onto the sheet pan.

8. While these look beautiful with a simple drizzle of chocolate on top, I do love the look of a fat, juicy raspberry perched on top. If you choose to do this, be sure that the raspberries have been completely dried before you top your truffles with them. The raspberries can go on top (carefully!) just after they've been dipped (chocolate should still be moist) and placed on the parchment lined sheet pan.

9. Just dipped in chocolate, these will last in an airtight container up to 3 weeks. With the raspberries on top, just a day or two!

CHINESE FIVE-SPICE TRUFFLES

Chinese five spice is a mix of flavors I really didn't get to know and appreciate until I had been in the chocolate business for years. I'm so glad my palate opened up to welcome this beautiful blend. It's really best in milk chocolate, in my opinion. Make sure your spices are fresh; if they sit around too long, they can lose potency.

This truffle is really perfect when dipped in milk chocolate. The richness of the spices really sings when they've got a little chocolate coat on top.

DAY ONE

What you'll need

2 ounces butter

¾ cup light cream

1½ pounds tempered milk chocolate

1¼ teaspoons Chinese five-spice mix

1. Over low heat, melt butter into cream in a heavy-bottomed sauce-pan. Use a small silicone spatula to stir gently all the while. When the butter has completely been incorporated into the cream, remove from heat.

2. Slowly pour a medium-sized stream of tempered chocolate into the cream and butter mixture, whisking constantly. When chocolate is completely mixed in, whisk in the spice.

3. Using a medium spatula, pour the truffle mixture into a parchment-lined, 9×9-inch baking pan.

4. Let cool completely, drape a piece of parchment paper over the top of the pan (do not wrap tightly—truffles need to breathe), and leave out at room temperature (not warmer than 70 degrees F) overnight.

What you'll need

½ pound tempered milk chocolate

Unsweetened cocoa for dusting hands, knife, truffles

3–5 pounds tempered milk chocolate in a bowl, for dipping
(I recommend you temper chocolate 1 pound at a time, to keep
it from going out of temper)

1. Using an offset spatula, spread ½ pound tempered chocolate over truffles in the 9×9-inch pan. Spread it as thinly and as uniformly as you can. Spread parchment paper over the wet chocolate. This will end up being the bottom of the truffle.

2. When chocolate is completely cooled and hard, lift truffles out of pan. Place the bottom of the pan on top of the cooled chocolate side (the bottom), and flip over carefully. Slide the truffles off the bottom of the pan onto your countertop. Carefully peel the parchment paper off the top of the truffle.

3. Lightly dust truffles with cocoa, then dust your hands and both sides of a chef's knife.

4. Score truffles with knife, looking to make 1×1-inch squares.

5. Cover both sides of the knife with cocoa, and cut a strip of truffles. Scrape the sides of the chef's knife with a butter knife, coat with cocoa, and cut another strip of truffles.

6. Cut into squares and place on a parchment-lined baking sheet. Continue cutting until all the truffles have been portioned out. Wipe the butter knife clean when finished; you'll need it again.

7. Place a truffle on your dipping fork. Tap lightly to dislodge any extra cocoa, then dip into the chocolate. After dipping, tap the fork gently on the side of the bowl to let any excess chocolate drip off. Using the butter knife to help with the transfer, tip the truffle onto the sheet pan.

8. When the truffle is still wet, lightly touch a top corner with two fingers, and then drag the strings of chocolate you've got on your fingertips across the top of the truffle diagonally to decorate.

9. These will last in an airtight container at room temperature 2 to 3 weeks.

WHITE CHOCOLATE LEMON TRUFFLES

The center of this truffle is made with white chocolate, but I like it dipped in dark. I tend to lean to dark chocolate when pairing with lemon, lime, or orange. The richness of the white chocolate serves as a perfect counterpoint to the tartness of the lemon. Simple and lovely.

DAY ONE

What you'll need

2 ounces butter

¾ cup light cream

1½ pounds tempered white chocolate

¾ teaspoon lemon extract (the best you can find!)

1. Over low heat, melt butter into cream. Use a small silicone spatula to stir gently all the while. When the butter has completely been incorporated into the cream, remove from heat.

2. Slowly pour a medium-sized stream of tempered chocolate into the cream and butter mixture, whisking constantly. When chocolate is completely mixed in, whisk in extract.

3. Using the medium spatula, pour the truffle mixture into a parchment-lined, 9×9-inch baking pan.

4. Let cool completely, drape a piece of parchment paper over the top of the pan, and leave out at room temperature (not warmer than 70 degrees F) overnight.

What you'll need

½ pound tempered dark chocolate

Unsweetened cocoa for dusting hands, knife, and truffles

3–5 pounds tempered dark chocolate in a bowl, for dipping
(I recommend you temper chocolate 1 pound at a time, to keep
it from going out of temper)

Sliced candied lemon peel, to decorate

1. Using an offset spatula, spread ½ pound tempered chocolate over truffles in the 9×9-inch pan. Spread it as thinly and as uniformly as you can. Spread parchment paper over the wet chocolate. This will end up being the bottom of the truffle.

2. When chocolate is completely cooled and hard, lift truffles out of pan. Place the bottom of the pan on top of the cooled chocolate side (the bottom), and flip over carefully. Slide the truffles off the bottom of the pan onto your countertop. Carefully peel the parchment paper off the top of the truffle.

3. Lightly dust truffles with cocoa, then dust your hands and both sides of a chef's knife.

4. Score truffles with knife, looking to make 1×1-inch squares.

5. Cover both sides of the knife with cocoa, and cut a strip of truffles. Scrape the sides of the chef's knife with a butter knife, coat with cocoa, and cut another strip of truffles.

6. Cut into squares and place on a parchment-lined baking sheet. Continue cutting until all the truffles have been portioned out. Wipe the butter knife clean when finished; you'll need it again.

7. Place a truffle on a dipping fork. Tap lightly to dislodge any extra cocoa, then dip into the tempered chocolate. After dipping, tap the fork gently on the side of the bowl to let any excess chocolate drip off. Using the butter knife to help with the transfer, tip the truffle onto the sheet pan.

8. When the truffle is still wet, carefully place a slice of candied lemon peel on the top of the truffle to decorate. When the chocolate is completely dry, place in candy cups and store in an airtight container. They're good for about 3 weeks.

MILK CHOCOLATE LAVENDER TRUFFLES

Lavender is a very subtle flavor, so these truffles are best in milk chocolate. What we want in this truffle is the hint of lavender, an insinuation of lavender. Too much can really seem soapy to me. I like being surprised by a peek of the flavor every now and then instead of being hit over the head with it. Choose the best quality dried lavender you can find. Don't use old stuff in the back of your cabinet—if you do, subtle flavor can easily turn into no flavor at all.

To keep those subtle flavors inside, we dip this in milk chocolate. Note there is an added step in day one, when we infuse the cream with lavender.

What you'll need

2 ½ teaspoons dried lavender

¾ cup light cream

2 ounces butter

1 ½ pounds tempered milk chocolate

1. Over low heat, bring lavender and cream to a simmer in a heavy-bottomed saucepan, stirring occasionally. When it comes to a simmer (don't let it boil!), stir a bit more, then remove from heat. Let the mixture cool.

2. When it's cool, strain the lavender from the cream with a small sieve into a 2-cup measuring cup.

3. Rinse the pan out, making sure there are no lavender solids remaining. Dry carefully.

4. Pour cream back into pan, and over low heat, melt butter into cream. Use a small silicone spatula to stir gently all the while. When the butter has completely been incorporated into the cream, remove from heat.

5. Slowly pour a medium-sized stream of tempered chocolate into the cream and butter mixture, whisking constantly.

6. Using the medium spatula, pour the truffle mixture into the parchment-lined, 9×9-inch baking pan.

7. Let cool completely, drape a piece of parchment paper over the top of the pan, and leave out at room temperature (not warmer than 70 degrees F) overnight.

What you'll need

½ pound tempered milk chocolate

Unsweetened cocoa for dusting hands, knife, and truffles

3–5 pounds tempered milk chocolate in a bowl for dipping (I recommend you temper chocolate 1 pound at a time, to keep it from going out of temper)

Candied violets, purple sprinkles, or pounded lavender mixed with a bit of sugar for decoration*

1. Using an offset spatula, spread ½ pound tempered chocolate over truffles in the 9×9-inch pan. Spread it as thinly and as uniformly as you can. Spread parchment paper over the wet chocolate. This will end up being the bottom of the truffle.

2. When chocolate is completely cooled and hard, lift truffles out of pan. Place the bottom of the pan on top of the cooled chocolate side (the bottom), and flip over carefully. Slide the truffles off the bottom of the pan onto your countertop. Carefully peel the parchment paper off the top of the truffle.

3. Lightly dust truffles with cocoa, then dust your hands and both sides of a chef's knife.

4. Score truffles with knife into 1×1-inch squares.

5. Cover both sides of the knife with cocoa and cut a strip of truffles. Scrape the sides of the chef's knife with a butter knife, coat with cocoa, and cut another strip of truffles.

6. Cut into squares, and place on a parchment-lined baking sheet. Continue cutting until all the truffles have been portioned out. Wipe the butter knife clean when finished; you'll need it again.

7. Place a truffle on a dipping fork. Tap lightly to dislodge any extra cocoa, then dip into the chocolate. After dipping, tap the fork gently on the side of the bowl to let any excess chocolate drip off. Using the butter knife to help with the transfer, tip the truffle onto the sheet pan.

8. When your truffles are still wet, top them with the decoration of your choice.

9. When completely dry, place in candy cups, and store in an airtight container for 2 to 3 weeks.

*Note: If you choose a dusting of lavender with sugar, crush ¼ teaspoon lavender in a mortar and pestle before mixing it with 1 tablespoon granulated sugar. Much more, and the soapy flavor may come into play.

SPICED PUMPKIN TRUFFLES

Autumn is in the air with this truffle. Pumpkin with a little spice is just the right duo of warm flavors to combine as the temperatures cool outside. I think the pumpkin wants to be dipped in milk chocolate, so it doesn't have to try too hard to be tasted.

DAY ONE

What you'll need

> 2 ounces butter
>
> ¾ cup light cream
>
> 1½ pounds tempered milk chocolate
>
> 2½ tablespoons pumpkin puree
>
> 1 teaspoon pumpkin spice mix:
>
> > ½ teaspoon cinnamon
> >
> > ¼ teaspoon ginger
> >
> > ⅛ teaspoon each nutmeg and allspice

1. Over low heat, melt butter into cream. Use a small silicone spatula to stir gently all the while. When the butter has completely been incorporated into the cream, remove from heat.

2. Slowly pour a medium-sized stream of tempered chocolate into the cream and butter mixture, whisking constantly. Make sure there are no lumps in your pumpkin puree, then whisk it into the truffle mix. Stir in spices.

3. Using a medium spatula, pour the truffle mixture into a parchment-lined, 9×9-inch baking pan.

4. Let cool completely, drape a piece of parchment paper over the top of the pan, and leave out at room temperature (not warmer than 70 degrees F) overnight.

What you'll need

½ pound tempered milk chocolate

Unsweetened cocoa for dusting hands, knife, and truffles

**3–5 pounds tempered milk chocolate in a bowl, for dipping
(I recommend you temper chocolate 1 pound at a time, to keep
it from going out of temper)**

1. Using an offset spatula, spread ½ pound tempered chocolate over truffles in the 9×9-inch pan. Spread it as thinly and as uniformly as you can. Spread parchment paper over the wet chocolate. This will end up being the bottom of the truffle.

2. When chocolate is completely cooled and hard, lift truffles out of pan. Place the bottom of the pan on top of the cooled chocolate side (the bottom), and flip over carefully. Slide the truffles off the bottom of the pan onto your countertop. Carefully peel the parchment paper off the top of the truffle.

3. Lightly dust truffles with cocoa, then dust your hands and both sides of a chef's knife.

4. Score truffles with knife, looking to make 1×1-inch squares.

5. Cover both sides of the knife with cocoa and cut a strip of truffles. Scrape the sides of the chef's knife with a butter knife, coat with cocoa, and cut another strip of truffles.

6. Cut into squares and place (with cocoa-covered fingers so they don't stick to you!) on parchment-lined baking sheet. Continue cutting until all the truffles have been portioned out. Wipe the butter knife clean when finished; you'll need it again.

7. Place a truffle on a dipping fork. Tap lightly to dislodge any extra cocoa, then dip into the tempered chocolate. After dipping, tap the fork gently on the side of the bowl to let any excess chocolate drip off. Using the butter knife to help with the transfer, tip the truffle onto the sheet pan. When the truffle is still wet, lightly touch the top with your pointer finger, and then draw a *P* with the string of chocolate you've got on your fingertip to decorate.

8. These will last in an airtight container for up to 2 weeks.

DARK MAYAN TRUFFLES

These really can be made in milk or dark. I prefer this flavor combination in dark, but you are welcome to experiment. I like these simply rolled, but if you want to dip them, you may (skip ahead to option two on day two). Make the truffle in one color, and dip in another, if you're feeling frisky.

The center of this truffle is a combination of a few flavors; very subtle, but round and full as a whole. These guys just taste better and better as the days go by; the flavors will intensify after a day or two.

DAY ONE

What you'll need

2 ounces butter

¾ cup light cream

1 ½ pounds tempered dark chocolate

1 teaspoon ancho chili powder

⅛ teaspoon cayenne

¼ teaspoon cinnamon

1. Over low heat, melt butter into cream in a heavy-bottomed saucepan. Use a small silicone spatula to stir gently. When the butter has completely melted into the cream, remove from heat.

2. Slowly pour a medium-sized stream of tempered chocolate into the cream and butter mixture, whisking constantly. When chocolate is fully incorporated, whisk in spices.

3. Using a medium spatula, pour the truffle mixture into a parchment-lined, 9×9-inch baking pan.

4. Let cool completely, loosely drape a piece of parchment paper over the top of the pan, and leave out at room temperature (not warmer than 70 degrees F) overnight.

Option one ♥ rolled truffles

2 tablespoons unsweetened cocoa

1 tablespoon sugar

½ teaspoon super finely ground coffee beans

Unsweetened cocoa for dusting hands and melon baller

1. Mix together cocoa, sugar, and coffee in a shallow bowl. Set aside.

2. Coat a melon baller in cocoa, then scoop truffle mixture into a ball. Drop ball into shallow bowl of cocoa mixture and roll around until completely covered. Place truffle on a parchment-lined baking sheet. Repeat until truffle mixture is used up.

3. When the truffles have rested for a bit, they can be put into candy cups and served, or stored in an airtight container for up to 1 week.

Option two ♥ cut truffles

½ pound tempered dark chocolate

Unsweetened cocoa for dusting hands, knife, and truffles

3–5 pounds tempered chocolate in a bowl, for dipping
(I recommend you temper chocolate 1 pound at a time, to keep
it from going out of temper)

1 tablespoon super finely ground coffee

1. Using an offset spatula, spread ½ pound tempered chocolate over truffles in the 9×9-inch pan. Spread it as thinly and as uniformly as you can. Spread parchment paper over the wet chocolate. This will end up being the bottom of the truffle.

2. When chocolate is completely cooled and hard, lift truffles out of pan. Place the bottom of the pan on top of the cooled chocolate side (the bottom), and flip over carefully. Slide the truffles off the bottom of the pan onto your countertop. Carefully peel the parchment paper off the top of the truffle.

3. Lightly dust truffles with cocoa, then dust your hands and both sides of a chef's knife.

4. Score truffles with knife, looking to make 1×1-inch squares.

5. Cover both sides of the knife with cocoa and cut a strip of truffles. Scrape the sides of the chef's knife with a butter knife, coat with cocoa, and cut another strip of truffles.

6. Cut into squares and place on a parchment-lined baking sheet. Continue cutting until all the truffles have been portioned out. Wipe the butter knife clean when finished; you'll need it again.

7. Place a truffle on a dipping fork. Tap lightly to dislodge any extra cocoa, then dip into the chocolate. After dipping, tap the fork gently on the side of the bowl to let any excess chocolate drip off. Using the butter knife to help with the transfer, tip the truffle onto the sheet pan.

8. When the truffle is still wet, lightly sprinkle coffee on top. Just a light sprinkle! These will last in an airtight container at room temperature for 2 weeks.

CARDAMOM-CINNAMON TRUFFLES

The Swiss have known for centuries what a beautiful combination cardamom and cinnamon make. The cardamom can be an elusive boost to the cinnamon; it's not so easy to pick out if done correctly. Have folks over when you make them—whoever guesses the flavors correctly gets a box to take home!

These, like most spiced truffles, are best dipped in chocolate. I prefer the dark for this, but if you prefer milk chocolate, go for it!

DAY ONE

What you'll need

2 ounces butter

¾ cup light cream

1½ pounds tempered chocolate

¾ teaspoon cinnamon

½ teaspoon cardamom

1. Over low heat, melt butter into cream in a heavy-bottomed saucepan. Use a small silicone spatula to stir gently all the while. When the butter has completely been incorporated into the cream, remove from heat.

2. Slowly pour a medium-sized stream of tempered chocolate into the cream and butter mixture, whisking constantly. When chocolate is completely mixed in, whisk in the spices.

3. Using a medium spatula, pour the truffle mixture into a parchment-lined, 9×9-inch baking pan.

4. Let cool completely, drape a piece of parchment paper over the top of the pan (do not wrap tightly!), and leave out at room temperature (not warmer than 70 degrees F) overnight.

What you'll need

½ pound tempered chocolate

Unsweetened cocoa for dusting hands, knife, and truffles

3–5 pounds tempered dark chocolate in a bowl, for dipping (I recommend you temper chocolate 1 pound at a time, to keep it from going out of temper)

1. Using an offset spatula, spread ½ pound tempered chocolate over truffles in the 9×9-inch pan. Spread it as thinly and as uniformly as you can. Spread parchment paper over the wet chocolate. This will end up being the bottom of the truffle.

2. When chocolate is completely cooled and hard, lift truffles out of pan. Place the bottom of the pan on top of the cooled chocolate side (the bottom), and flip over carefully. Slide the truffles off the bottom of the pan onto your countertop. Carefully peel the parchment paper off the top of the truffle.

3. Lightly dust truffles with cocoa, then dust your hands and both sides of a chef's knife.

4. Score truffles with knife, looking to make 1×1-inch squares.

5. Cover both sides of the knife with cocoa and cut a strip of truffles. Scrape the sides of the chef's knife with a butter knife, coat with cocoa, and cut another strip of truffles.

6. Cut into squares and place on a parchment-lined baking sheet. Continue cutting until all the truffles have been portioned out. Wipe the butter knife clean when finished; you'll need it again.

7. Place a truffle on your dipping fork. Tap lightly to dislodge any extra cocoa, then dip into the chocolate. After dipping, tap the fork gently on the side of the bowl to let any excess chocolate drip off. Using the butter knife to help with the transfer, tip the truffle onto the sheet pan.

8. When the truffle is still wet, lightly touch the top with your pointer finger, and then draw a C with the string of chocolate you've got on your fingertip to decorate.

9. These will last in an airtight container at room temperature 2 to 3 weeks.

DARK CHOCOLATE-DIPPED WHITE STRAWBERRY TRUFFLES

Strawberry puree whipped into a white chocolate truffle center is a decadent and beautiful surprise when biting into a dark chocolate–dipped truffle. The white chocolate's silkiness heightens the sweet-tart of the strawberry, and the color contrast between the center and the chocolate coating is stunning.

If you want to keep it simple, just stick with one type of chocolate. The recipe is written for the full monty, but feel free to stay mono on this one if you prefer.

DAY ONE

What you'll need

2 ounces butter

¾ cup light cream

1½ pounds tempered white chocolate

2½ teaspoons strawberry puree

1. Over low heat, melt butter into cream in a heavy-bottomed saucepan. Use a small silicone spatula to stir gently all the while. When the butter has completely been incorporated into the cream, remove from heat.

2. Slowly pour a medium-sized stream of tempered chocolate into the cream and butter mixture, whisking constantly. When chocolate is completely mixed in, and after ensuring that there are no lumps in your strawberry puree, whisk the puree in.

3. Using a medium spatula, pour the truffle mixture into a parchment-lined 9×9-inch baking pan.

4. Let cool completely. Loosely drape a piece of parchment paper over the top of the pan, and leave out at room temperature (not warmer than 70 degrees F) overnight.

What you'll need

½ pound tempered dark chocolate

Unsweetened cocoa for dusting hands, knife, and truffles

**3–5 pounds tempered dark chocolate in a bowl, for dipping
(I recommend you temper chocolate 1 pound at a time, to keep
it from going out of temper)**

Freeze-dried strawberry slices to decorate, optional

1. Using an offset spatula, spread ½ pound tempered chocolate over truffles in the 9×9-inch pan. Spread it as thinly and as uniformly as you can. Spread parchment paper over the wet chocolate. This will end up being the bottom of the truffle.

2. When chocolate is completely cooled and hard, lift truffles out of pan. Place the bottom of the pan on top of the cooled chocolate side (the bottom), and flip over carefully. Slide the truffles off the bottom of the pan onto your countertop. Carefully peel the parchment paper off the top of the truffle.

3. Lightly dust truffles with cocoa, then dust your hands and both sides of a chef's knife.

4. Score truffles with knife, looking to make 1×1-inch squares.

5. Cover both sides of the knife with cocoa and cut a strip of truffles. Scrape the sides of the chef's knife with a butter knife, coat with cocoa, and cut another strip of truffles.

6. Cut into squares and place on a parchment-lined baking sheet. Continue cutting until all the truffles have been portioned out. Wipe the butter knife clean when finished; you'll need it again.

7. Place a truffle on a dipping fork. Tap lightly to dislodge any extra cocoa, then dip into the tempered chocolate. After dipping, tap the fork gently on the side of the bowl to let any excess chocolate drip off. Using the butter knife to help with the transfer, tip the truffle onto the sheet pan.

8. When the truffle is still wet, carefully place a slice of freeze-dried strawberry on the top of the truffle to decorate.

9. These will last in an airtight container at room temperature 3 weeks.

resources

AMAZON

www.amazon.com

Candy funnel, 2 oz. scoop, tempered glass bowls, chocolate spatula thermometer, offset spatula, sheet pan, just about everything but the kitchen sink! Very competitive pricing.

KING ARTHUR FLOUR

www.kingarthurflour.com

1.800.827. 6836

Parchment paper, decorating sugars and sprinkles, extracts, cocoa powder, premade caramel, great prices and quality.

CHOCOSPHERE

www.chocosphere.com

877-992-4626 / 503-692-3323

Chocolate, blocks size to discs, many different manufacturers, decorations, nut pastes, flavors, fruits large variety.

JB PRINCE COMPANY

www.jbprince.com

Cookware, utensils (dipping forks, offset spatulas, funnels), tends toward a more professional crowd.

Great if you intend to use your tools heavily.

GYGI

www.gygi.com

Premade Caramel, Chocolate blocks to discs, utensils, cocoa

PENZEYS

www.penzeys.com

1.800.741.7787

Spices, herbs, best quality.

ARCADE SNACKS

www.arcadesnacks.com

800-370-7070

Dried fruits, roasted nuts, raw nuts, super fresh and tasty!

SUPERIOR NUT

www.superiornut.com

(617) 876-3808

Roasted and raw nuts, almonds are to die for.

LA CUISINE

www.lacuisineus.com

800.521.1176

Utensils, high quality chocolate, cocoa powder

CHOCOLEY

www.chocoley.com

866.528.5252

Chocolate, utensils, caramel, extracts and flavorings, decorative sugars and sprinkles, fun tips and easy to shop.

acknowledgements

Deepest thanks and sympathy to Graham and Sheila for experiencing all the ups and downs of this process. Mwah!

Many thanks to Hollan Publishing for calling me up and convincing me this was a good idea.

Thank you to Countryman Press and W. W. Norton and Co. Huge thanks to Ann Treistman, my editor, who never once made me feel like the novice writer I am.

Thank you to my family, past and present, blood and chosen, for constant support, red wine, fresh-grown veggies, open ears and hearts: Grandma Schlosser, Mom, Dad, Cody, Annie, and Ben, Lauren, Ron, Caleb and Esme, Evan and Casey, the Lyman brothers, Chuck and Chris, Jill, Jennie the Boots, Cassie, Niaz, Vivien, LeRoy, Miss Margot Isabelle, Laurie and Jay, and all the folks who have helped at Turtle Alley, loved Turtle Alley, and supported it since it was just a baby. I'm going to forget people, and they are going to forgive me. Because you like me! You really like me!

index